our best KNIT BABY AFGHANS

*T*he arrival of a precious newborn is a joyous time for all. With gifts in hand, family and friends wait excitedly for their first glimpse of the baby and for the chance to shower the little one with love. You'll find the perfect "birth-day" present in Our Best Knit Baby Afghans, a collection of 33 darling cover-ups for sweet little misses and bouncing baby boys. Fashioned in baby-soft yarns, the designs range from classic ripples and blossoming flowers to rich diamonds and lacy heirloom creations. And our close-up photos and clear instructions make them all fun to knit! So go ahead and knit a keepsake that Mom and Baby will love for a lifetime.

LEISURE ARTS, INC.
Little Rock, Arkansas

EDITORIAL STAFF

Editor-at-Large: Anne Van Wagner Childs
Vice President and Editor-in-Chief: Sandra Graham Case
Editorial Director: Susan Frantz Wiles
Publications Director: Susan White Sullivan
Creative Art Director: Gloria Bearden
Photography Director: Karen Hall
Art Operations Director: Jeff Curtis

PRODUCTION
Technical Editors: Cathy Hardy, Lois J. Long, and Linda Luder
Senior Instructional Editor: Valesha Kirksey
Instructional Editors: Susan Ackerman Carter, Sue Galucki, and Sarah J. Green

EDITORIAL
Managing Editor: Tammi Williamson Bradley
Associate Editors: Darla Burdette Kelsay and Jennifer L. Riley

ART
Graphics Art Director: Rhonda Hodge Shelby
Senior Graphics Illustrator: Lora Puls
Graphics Illustrator: Dana Vaughn
Color Technician: Mark Hawkins
Photography Stylists: Sondra Daniel and Tiffany Huffman

BUSINESS STAFF

Publisher: Rick Barton
Vice President, Finance: Tom Siebenmorgen
Vice President, Retail Marketing: Bob Humphrey
Director of Corporate Planning and Development: Laticia Mull Cornett
Vice President, National Accounts: Pam Stebbins
Retail Marketing Director: Margaret Sweetin
General Merchandise Manager: Cathy Laird
Vice President, Operations: Jim Dittrich
Distribution Director: Rob Thieme
Retail Customer Service Manager: Wanda Price
Print Production Manager: Fred F. Pruss

2

TABLE OF CONTENTS

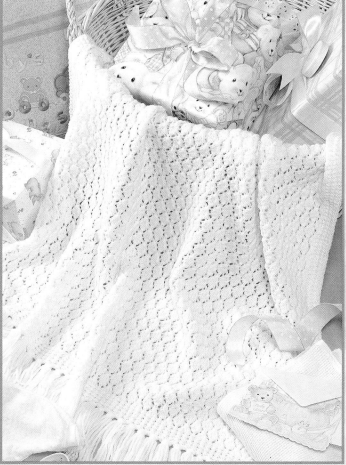

PRECIOUS IN PINK

Lacy hearts accentuate this precious pink throw. The heartwarming wrap offers a sweet way to express your sentiments for an adorable little miss.

Finished Size: 32" x 44"

MATERIALS
Sport Weight Yarn:
13 ounces, (370 grams, 1,225 yards)
24" Circular knitting needle, size 7 (4.50 mm)
or size needed for gauge

GAUGE: In Stockinette Stitch,
20 sts and 26 rows = 4"

AFGHAN
Cast on 150 sts.

Rows 1-10: Knit across.

Row 11: K5, P 10, ★ increase *(see Increases, page 77)*, P 12; repeat from ★ across to last 5 sts, K5: 160 sts.

Row 12 (Right side)**:** Knit across.

Row 13: K5, purl across to last 5 sts, K5.

Rows 14-21: Repeat Rows 12 and 13, 4 times.

Row 22: K 27, YO *(Fig. 4a, page 77)*, SSK *(Figs. 13a-c, page 79)*, (K 33, YO, SSK) 3 times, K 26.

Row 23 AND ALL WRONG SIDE ROWS THRU Row 53: K5, purl across to last 5 sts, K5.

Row 24: K 25, K2 tog *(Fig. 5, page 78)*, YO, K1 tbl *(Fig. 3a, page 77)*, YO, SSK, (K 30, K2 tog, YO, K1 tbl, YO, SSK) 3 times, K 25.

Row 26: K 24, K2 tog, YO, K1 tbl, (YO, SSK) twice, ★ K 28, K2 tog, YO, K1 tbl, (YO, SSK) twice; repeat from ★ 2 times **more**, K 24.

Row 28: K 23, (K2 tog, YO) twice, K1 tbl, (YO, SSK) twice, ★ K 26, (K2 tog, YO) twice, K1 tbl, (YO, SSK) twice; repeat from ★ 2 times **more**, K 23.

Row 30: K 22, (K2 tog, YO) twice, K1 tbl, (YO, SSK) 3 times, ★ K 24, (K2 tog, YO) twice, K1 tbl, (YO, SSK) 3 times; repeat from ★ 2 times **more**, K 22.

Row 32: K 21, (K2 tog, YO) 3 times, K1 tbl, (YO, SSK) 3 times, ★ K 22, (K2 tog, YO) 3 times, K1 tbl, (YO, SSK) 3 times; repeat from ★ 2 times **more**, K 21.

Row 34: K 20, ★ (K2 tog, YO) 3 times, K1 tbl, (YO, SSK) 4 times, K 20; repeat from ★ across.

Row 36: K 19, (K2 tog, YO) 4 times, K1 tbl, (YO, SSK) 4 times, ★ K 18, (K2 tog, YO) 4 times, K1 tbl, (YO, SSK) 4 times; repeat from ★ 2 times **more**, K 19.

Row 38: K 18, (K2 tog, YO) 4 times, K1 tbl, (YO, SSK) 5 times, ★ K 16, (K2 tog, YO) 4 times, K1 tbl, (YO, SSK) 5 times; repeat from ★ 2 times **more**, K 18.

Row 40: K 17, (K2 tog, YO) 3 times, K1 tbl, YO, SSK, YO, [slip 1, K2 tog, PSSO *(Figs. 12a & b, page 79)*], YO, K2 tog, YO, K1 tbl, (YO, SSK) 3 times, ★ K 14, (K2 tog, YO) 3 times, K1 tbl, YO, SSK, YO, slip 1, K2 tog, PSSO, YO, K2 tog, YO, K1 tbl, (YO, SSK) 3 times; repeat from ★ 2 times **more**, K 17.

Row 42: K 16, (K2 tog, YO) 3 times, K1 tbl, YO, SSK, YO, slip 1, K2 tog, PSSO, YO, (K2 tog, YO) twice, K1 tbl, (YO, SSK) 3 times, ★ K 12, (K2 tog, YO) 3 times, K1 tbl, YO, SSK, YO, slip 1, K2 tog, PSSO, YO, (K2 tog, YO) twice, K1 tbl, (YO, SSK) 3 times; repeat from ★ 2 times **more**, K 16.

Row 44: K 15, (K2 tog, YO) 3 times, K1 tbl, YO, (SSK, YO) twice, slip 1, K2 tog, PSSO, YO, (SSK, YO) twice, K1 tbl, (YO, SSK) 3 times, ★ K 10, (K2 tog, YO) 3 times, K1 tbl, YO, (SSK, YO) twice, slip 1, K2 tog, PSSO, YO, (SSK, YO) twice, K1 tbl, (YO, SSK) 3 times; repeat from ★ 2 times **more**, K 15.

Row 46: K 16, YO, (K2 tog, YO) twice, slip 1, K2 tog, PSSO, YO, (SSK, YO) twice, K1 tbl, YO, (K2 tog, YO) twice, slip 1, K2 tog, PSSO, YO, (SSK, YO) twice, ★ K 12, YO, (K2 tog, YO) twice, slip 1, K2 tog, PSSO, YO, (SSK, YO) twice, K1 tbl, YO, (K2 tog, YO) twice, slip 1, K2 tog, PSSO, YO, (SSK, YO) twice; repeat from ★ 2 times **more**, K 16.

Continued on page 72.

SWEET AND SIMPLE

Need a shower gift in a hurry? With its simplistic styling, this sleepytime afghan works up in a jiffy! A lattice-look fringe lends a decorative finish.

Finished Size: 32" x 42"

MATERIALS
Sport Weight Yarn:
   13 ounces, (370 grams, 1,635 yards)
29" Circular knitting needle, size 6 (4.00 mm)
   or size needed for gauge
Crochet hook for fringe

GAUGE: In pattern, 18 sts and 24 rows = 4"

See Yarn Overs, page 77, before beginning.

AFGHAN
Cast on 146 sts.

Rows 1-6: Purl across.

Row 7 (Right side)**:** P4, ★ YO, K2 tog *(Fig. 5, page 78)*; repeat from ★ across to last 4 sts, P4.

Row 8: Purl across.

Row 9: P4, (K2 tog, YO) across to last 4 sts, P4.

Rows 10-12: Purl across.

Row 13: P4, (YO, K2 tog) across to last 4 sts, P4.

Repeat Rows 8-13 for pattern until Afghan measures approximately 41" from cast on edge, ending by working Row 9.

Last 6 Rows: Purl across.

Bind off all sts in **purl**.

Holding seven 18" lengths of yarn together, add fringe evenly across short edges of Afghan through Step 3 *(see Fringe, page 80)*.

Design by Jean Lampe.

DAINTY DAISIES

Dotted with dainty yellow "daisies," this pristine throw gets its pretty pattern from rows of openwork triangles.

Finished Size: 30" x 35½"

MATERIALS

Sport Weight Yarn:
    White - 13 ounces, (370 grams, 1,225 yards)
    Yellow - ¾ ounce, (20 grams, 70 yards)
24" Circular knitting needle, size 5 (3.75 mm)
    or size needed for gauge
Tapestry needle
Crochet hook for fringe

GAUGE: In Stockinette Stitch,
        22 sts and 30 rows = 4"

AFGHAN

With White, cast on 165 sts.

Rows 1 and 2: Knit across.

Row 3 (Right side)**:** K5, ★ K2 tog *(Fig. 5, page 78)*, YO *(Fig. 4a, page 77)*, K6; repeat from ★ across.

Row 4: K2, purl across to last 2 sts, K2.

Row 5: K4, K2 tog, YO, K1, YO, [slip 1, K1, PSSO *(Fig. 10, page 78)*], ★ K3, K2 tog, YO, K1, YO, slip 1, K1, PSSO; repeat from ★ across to last 4 sts, K4.

Row 6: K2, purl across to last 2 sts, K2.

Row 7: K3, K2 tog, YO, K3, YO, slip 1, K1, PSSO, ★ K1, K2 tog, YO, K3, YO, slip 1, K1, PSSO; repeat from ★ across to last 3 sts, K3.

Row 8: K2, purl across to last 2 sts, K2.

Row 9: K2, K2 tog, YO, K1, ★ YO, [slip 1, K2 tog, PSSO *(Figs. 12a & b, page 79)*], YO, K1; repeat from ★ across to last 4 sts, YO, slip 1, K1, PSSO, K2.

Row 10: K2, purl across to last 2 sts, K2.

Rows 11-15: Knit across.

Row 16: K2, purl across to last 2 sts, K2.

Rows 17-20: Repeat Rows 15 and 16 twice.

Rows 21-24: Knit across.

Repeat Rows 3-24 for pattern until Afghan measures approximately 35½" from cast on edge, ending by working Row 12.

Bind off all sts in **knit**.

EMBROIDERY

With Yellow and using photo as a guide for placement:
Add ten 6-petal Lazy Daisy Stitch flowers in first Stockinette Stitch section of Afghan *(Fig. 19, page 80)*.
Add nine 6-petal Lazy Daisy Stitch flowers in next Stockinette Stitch section.
Continue in same manner, alternating 9 and 10 flowers for each remaining Stockinette Stitch section.

Holding four 16" lengths of White yarn together, add fringe evenly across short edges of Afghan through Step 1 *(see Fringe, page 80)*.

Design by Brooke Shellflower.

LILAC LOVELINESS

Wrapped in this splendid throw, your little prince or princess will feel like royalty!
Rich, lacy panels and lavender accents give it majestic magnificence.

Finished Size: 31" x 36" (before Embroidery)

MATERIALS

Sport Weight Yarn:
   White - 10 ounces, (280 grams, 945 yards)
   Lavender - 3/4 ounce, (20 grams, 70 yards)
24" Circular knitting needle, size 6 (4.00 mm)
   or size needed for gauge
Tapestry needle

GAUGE: In Stockinette Stitch,
         21 sts and 28 rows = 4"

See Yarn Overs and Decreases, pages 77-79, before beginning.

AFGHAN

With White, cast on 172 sts.

Rows 1 and 2: Knit across.

Row 3 (Right side)**:** K4, P2, ★ K5, (K2 tog, YO) twice, SSK, K5, P2; repeat from ★ across to last 4 sts, K4: 163 sts.

Row 4: K2, P2, K2, ★ P4, P2 tog tbl, YO, P1, increase **(see Increases, page 77)**, P1, YO, P2 tog, P4, K2; repeat from ★ across to last 4 sts, P2, K2: 172 sts.

Row 5: K4, P2, ★ K3, K2 tog, YO, K6, YO, SSK, K3, P2; repeat from ★ across to last 4 sts, K4.

Row 6: (K2, P2) twice, ★ P2 tog tbl, YO, P8, YO, P2 tog, P2, K2, P2; repeat from ★ across to last 2 sts, K2.

Row 7: K4, P2, ★ K3, YO, K3, K2 tog, SSK, K3, YO, K3, P2; repeat from ★ across to last 4 sts, K4.

Row 8: K2, P2, K2, ★ P4, YO, P2, P2 tog tbl, P2 tog, P2, YO, P4, K2; repeat from ★ across to last 4 sts, P2, K2.

Row 9: K4, P2, ★ K5, YO, K1, K2 tog, SSK, K1, YO, K5, P2; repeat from ★ across to last 4 sts, K4.

Row 10: K2, P2, K2, ★ P6, YO, P2 tog tbl, P2 tog, YO, P6, K2; repeat from ★ across to last 4 sts, P2, K2.

Repeat Rows 3-10 for pattern until Afghan measures approximately 35 1/2" from cast on edge, ending by working Row 10.

Last 2 Rows: Knit across.

Bind off all sts in **knit**.

EMBROIDERY

Using photo as a guide for placement, add embroidery to Afghan as follows:
With a double strand of Lavender, work Bullion Knot (wrapping 4 times) along center of each lace section **(Fig. 17, page 80)**.

With a double strand of Lavender, weave under and over 2 rows along first purl stitch of Reverse Stockinette section (located on either side of each lace section). Repeat along second purl stitch, alternating weaving.

Design by Brooke Shellflower.

FANCIFUL ROSE

This rosy cover-up is destined to be a family favorite. Fashioned in worsted weight yarn, it features a fanciful pattern with decidedly feminine appeal.

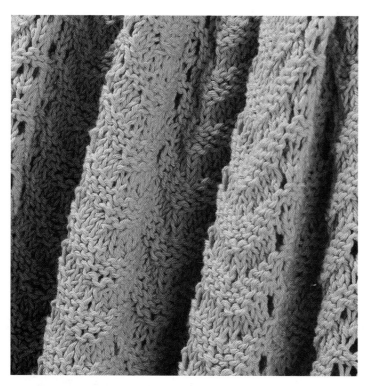

Finished Size: 35" x 41"

MATERIALS
Worsted Weight Yarn:
  22 ounces, (620 grams, 970 yards)
  29" Circular knitting needle, size 10 (6.00 mm)
    or size needed for gauge

GAUGE: In Stockinette Stitch,
        16 sts and 20 rows = 4"

AFGHAN
Cast on 140 sts.

Row 1: K4, K2 tog *(Fig. 5, page 78)*, K3, YO *(Fig. 4a, page 77)*, K1, YO, K3, ★ K2 tog twice, K3, YO, K1, YO, K3; repeat from ★ across to last 6 sts, K2 tog, K4.

Row 2: K4, purl across to last 4 sts, K4.

Row 3: Knit across.

Row 4: K4, K2 tog, K3, YO, K1, YO, K3, ★ K2 tog twice, K3, YO, K1, YO, K3; repeat from ★ across to last 6 sts, K2 tog, K4.

Repeat Rows 2-4 for pattern until Afghan measures approximately 41" from cast on edge, ending by working Row 2.

Bind off all sts in pattern.

Design by Rachel J. Terrill.

"MINT" FOR FRIENDS

Luxurious texture adds a merry touch to this cheery wrap knitted in soothing mint.
Rows of textured stitches create the illusion of children holding hands.

Finished Size: 33" x 37¹/₂"

MATERIALS

Sport Weight Yarn:
  13 ounces, (370 grams, 1,225 yards)
  24" Circular knitting needle, size 7 (4.50 mm)
    or size needed for gauge

GAUGE: In Stockinette Stitch,
    20 sts and 26 rows = 4"

STITCH GUIDE

BOBBLE (uses one st)
(K, P, K) **all** in next st, **turn**; K3, **turn**; K3, slip second and third sts on right needle over first st and off needle.

AFGHAN

Cast on 167 sts.

Rows 1-9: K1, (P1, K1) across.

Row 10 (Right side)**:** Knit across.

Row 11: Purl across.

Rows 12 and 13: Repeat Rows 10 and 11.

When instructed to slip a stitch, always slip as if to **purl**.

Row 14: P4, WYF slip 3, (P3, WYF slip 3) across to last 4 sts, P4.

Row 15: K4, WYB slip 3, (K3, WYB slip 3) across to last 4 sts, K4.

Row 16: Knit across.

Row 17: Purl across.

Row 18: K5, ★ insert right needle under loose strands and knit together with next st *(Fig. A)*, K5 repeat from ★ across.

Fig. A

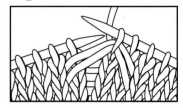

Row 19: Purl across.

Row 20: K5, (work Bobble, K5) across.

Row 21: Purl across.

Row 22: Knit across.

Row 23: Purl across.

Rows 24-33: Repeat Rows 14-23.

Rows 34-43: K1, (P1, K1) across.

Repeat Rows 10-43 for pattern until Afghan measures approximately 37¹/₂" from cast on edge, ending by working Row 43.

Bind off all sts in pattern.

Design by Brooke Shellflower.

SUNNY CABLES AND FEATHERS

Beautifully detailed, this cozy cover-up will escort baby in style to any occasion that demands dressing up. Only baby's first smiles will outshine its sunny radiance.

Finished Size: 35" x 42"

MATERIALS

Worsted Weight Yarn:
23 ounces, (650 grams, 1,010 yards)
29" Circular knitting needle, size 10 (6.00 mm)
or size needed for gauge
Cable needle

GAUGE: In Stockinette Stitch,
16 sts and 20 rows = 4"

STITCH GUIDE

CABLE (uses 6 sts)
Slip next 3 sts onto cable needle and hold in **back** of work, K3 from left needle, K3 from cable needle.

AFGHAN

Cast on 137 sts.

Rows 1-7: Knit across.

Row 8 (Right side)**:** Knit across increasing 30 sts evenly spaced **(see Increasing Evenly Across A Row, page 77)**: 167 sts.

Row 9: K4, purl across to last 4 sts, K4.

Row 10: K7, K2 tog 3 times **(Fig. 5, page 78)**, YO **(Fig. 4a, page 77)**, (K1, YO) 5 times, ★ K2 tog 6 times, YO, (K1, YO) 5 times; repeat from ★ across to last 13 sts, K2 tog 3 times, K7.

Row 11: K4, P6, (K 11, P6) across to last 4 sts, K4.

Row 12: K4, work Cable, (K 11, work Cable) across to last 4 sts, K4.

Row 13: K4, purl across to last 4 sts, K4.

Row 14: K7, K2 tog 3 times, YO, (K1, YO) 5 times, ★ K2 tog 6 times, YO, (K1, YO) 5 times; repeat from ★ across to last 13 sts, K2 tog 3 times, K7.

Row 15: K4, P6, (K 11, P6) across to last 4 sts, K4.

Row 16: Knit across.

Repeat Rows 9-16 for pattern until Afghan measures approximately 41" from cast on edge, ending by working Row 12.

Next Row: Knit across decreasing 30 sts evenly spaced: 137 sts.

Last 6 Rows: Knit across.

Bind off all sts in **knit**.

Design by Rachel J. Terrill.

A SHOWER OF LOVE

You'll be showered with "oohs" and "aahs" when you fashion this enchanting rock-a-bye wrap for a shower gift. The delightful design will please Mother and Baby alike.

Finished Size: 32" x 38"

MATERIALS

Sport Weight Yarn:
    White - 14$\frac{1}{2}$ ounces,
      (410 grams, 1,370 yards)
    Blue - $\frac{1}{2}$ ounce, (15 grams, 50 yards)
24" Circular knitting needle, size 5 (3.75 mm)
    or size needed for gauge
Cable needle
Tapestry needle

GAUGE: In Seed Stitch, 22 sts and 40 rows = 4"

STITCH GUIDE

> **CABLE** (uses 6 sts)
> Slip next 3 sts onto cable needle and hold in **back** of work, K3 from left needle, K3 from cable needle.

AFGHAN

With White, cast on 179 sts.

Rows 1-10: K1, (P1, K1) across.

Row 11 AND ALL WRONG SIDE ROWS: K1, (P1, K1) twice, purl across to last 5 sts, K1, (P1, K1) twice.

Row 12 (Right side)**:** K1, (P1, K1) 3 times, YO *(Fig. 4a, page 77)*, SSK *(Figs. 13a-c, page 79)*, K1, K2 tog *(Fig. 5, page 78)*, ★ YO, K2, increase *(see Increases, page 77)*, K2, YO, SSK, K1, K2 tog; repeat from ★ across to last 7 sts, YO, K1, (P1, K1) 3 times: 195 sts.

Row 14: (K1, P1) 3 times, K2, YO, [slip 1, K2 tog, PSSO *(Figs. 12a & b, page 79)*], ★ YO, K1, work Cable, K1, YO, slip 1, K2 tog, PSSO; repeat from ★ across to last 8 sts, YO, K2, (P1, K1) 3 times.

Row 16: K1, (P1, K1) 3 times, YO, SSK, K1, K2 tog, ★ YO, K6, YO, SSK, K1, K2 tog; repeat from ★ across to last 7 sts, YO, K1, (P1, K1) 3 times.

Row 18: (K1, P1) 3 times, K2, YO, slip 1, K2 tog, PSSO, ★ YO, K8, YO, slip 1, K2 tog, PSSO; repeat from ★ across to last 8 sts, YO, K2, (P1, K1) 3 times.

Row 20: K1, (P1, K1) 3 times, YO, SSK, K1, K2 tog, ★ YO, K6, YO, SSK, K1, K2 tog; repeat from ★ across to last 7 sts, YO, K1, (P1, K1) 3 times.

Row 21: K1, (P1, K1) twice, purl across to last 5 sts, K1, (P1, K1) twice.

Repeat Rows 14-21 for pattern until Afghan measures approximately 37" from cast on edge, ending by working Row 19.

Next Row: K1, (P1, K1) 3 times, YO, SSK, K1, K2 tog, ★ YO, K2, K2 tog, K2, YO, SSK, K1, K2 tog; repeat from ★ across to last 7 sts, YO, K1, (P1, K1) 3 times: 179 sts.

Last 9 Rows: K1, (P1, K1) across.

Bind off all sts in pattern.

EMBROIDERY

With a double strand of Blue and using photo as a guide for placement, add one French Knot to the center of each Cable *(Fig. 18, page 80)*.

Design by Brooke Shellflower.

NURSERY NECESSITY

A must-have for the nursery, this homespun cover features a solid weave that's warm and durable. A decorative finish gives the wrap classic character.

Finished Size: 35" x 46"

MATERIALS
Sport Weight Yarn:
   18 ounces, (510 grams, 1,700 yards)
24" Circular knitting needle, size 6 (4.00 mm)
   or size needed for gauge
Crochet hook for fringe

GAUGE: In pattern, 21 sts and 36 rows = 4"

AFGHAN
Cast on 186 sts.

Row 1 (Right side)**:** (K1, P1) twice, K2, ★ YO *(Fig. 4a, page 77)*, [slip 1, K1, PSSO *(Fig. 10, page 78)*], K2; repeat from ★ across to last 4 sts, (P1, K1) twice.

Row 2: Slip 1 as if to **purl**, P1, K1, P1, YO *(Fig. 4b, page 77)*, P2 tog *(Fig. 8, page 78)*, ★ P2, YO, P2 tog; repeat from ★ across to last 4 sts, P1, K1, P2.

Row 3: Slip 1 as if to **knit**, P1, K1, P1, K2, ★ YO, slip 1, K1, PSSO, K2; repeat from ★ across to last 4 sts, (P1, K1) twice.

Row 4: Slip 1 as if to **purl**, P1, K1, P1, YO, P2 tog, ★ P2, YO, P2 tog; repeat from ★ across to last 4 sts, P1, K1, P2.

Rows 5-12: Repeat Rows 3 and 4, 4 times.

Row 13: Slip 1 as if to **knit**, P1, K1, P1, increase *(see Increases, page 77)*, knit across to last 4 sts, (P1, K1) twice: 187 sts.

Row 14: Slip 1 as if to **purl**, P1, K1, purl across to last 3 sts, K1, P2.

Row 15: Slip 1 as if to **knit**, P1, K1, P1, K3, P1, K1, P1, ★ (K3, P1) twice, K1, P1; repeat from ★ across to last 7 sts, K3, (P1, K1) twice.

Row 16: Slip 1 as if to **purl**, P1, K1, P5, K1, P3, K1, P1, K1, ★ (P3, K1) twice, P1, K1; repeat from ★ across to last 12 sts, P3, K1, P5, K1, P2.

Row 17: Slip 1 as if to **knit**, P1, K1, P1, K7, P1, (K1, P1) twice, ★ K5, P1, (K1, P1) twice; repeat from ★ across to last 11 sts, K7, (P1, K1) twice.

Row 18: Slip 1 as if to **purl**, P1, K1, P7, K1, (P1, K1) 3 times, ★ P3, K1, (P1, K1) 3 times; repeat from ★ across to last 10 sts, P7, K1, P2.

Row 19: Repeat Row 17.

Row 20: Repeat Row 16.

Row 21: Repeat Row 15.

Row 22: Slip 1 as if to **purl**, P1, K1, P3, K1, (P1, K1) twice, ★ P5, K1, (P1, K1) twice; repeat from ★ across to last 6 sts, P3, K1, P2.

Row 23: Slip 1 as if to **knit**, P1, (K1, P1) 5 times, K3, ★ P1, (K1, P1) 3 times, K3; repeat from ★ across to last 12 sts, (P1, K1) across.

Row 24: Slip 1 as if to **purl**, P1, K1, P3, K1, (P1, K1) twice, ★ P5, K1, (P1, K1) twice; repeat from ★ across to last 6 sts, P3, K1, P2.

Repeat Rows 15-24 for pattern until Afghan measures approximately 43" from cast on edge, ending by working Row 22.

Next Row: Slip 1 as if to **knit**, P1, K1, P1, K2 tog *(Fig. 5, page 78)*, knit across to last 4 sts, (P1, K1) twice: 186 sts.

Next Row: Slip 1 as if to **purl**, P1, K1, purl across to last 3 sts, K1, P2.

Last 12 Rows: Repeat Rows 3 and 4, 6 times.

Bind off all sts in **knit**.

Holding five 18" lengths of yarn together, add fringe evenly across short edges of Afghan through Step 3 *(see Fringe, page 80)*.

Design by Shobha Govindan.

PURE WHITE PLEASER

You can never have too many snuggly covers, especially when they're as wonderful as this one is! Knitted in pure white, this inviting throw is ideal for boys and girls.

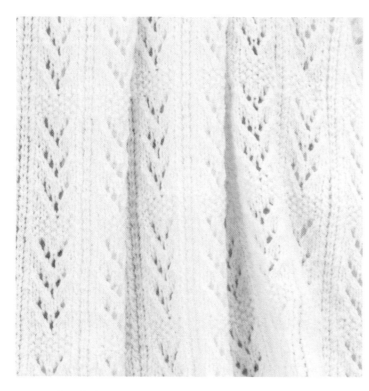

Finished Size: 31" x 43"

MATERIALS
Sport Weight Yarn:
 11 ounces, (310 grams, 1,385 yards)
 29" Circular knitting needle, size 6 (4.00 mm)
  or size needed for gauge

GAUGE: In Seed Stitch, 20 sts and 28 rows = 4"

AFGHAN
Cast on 171 sts.

Rows 1-8: K1, (P1, K1) across.

Row 9 (Right side)**:** K1, (P1, K1) twice, K2 tog *(Fig. 5, page 78)*, YO *(Fig. 4a, page 77)*, K1, YO, [slip 1, K1, PSSO *(Fig. 10, page 78)*], ★ K3, YO, slip 1, K1, PSSO, K2, K2 tog, YO, K1, YO, slip 1, K1, PSSO; repeat from ★ across to last 5 sts, K1, (P1, K1) twice.

Row 10: K1, (P1, K1) twice, purl across to last 5 sts, K1, (P1, K1) twice.

Row 11: K1, (P1, K1) twice, ★ K2 tog, YO, K1, YO, slip 1, K1, PSSO, K1; repeat from ★ across to last 4 sts, (P1, K1) twice.

Row 12: K1, (P1, K1) twice, purl across to last 5 sts, K1, (P1, K1) twice.

Row 13: K1, (P1, K1) twice, K2 tog, YO, K1, YO, slip 1, K1, PSSO, ★ K2 tog, YO, K3, YO, slip 1, K1, PSSO, K2 tog, YO, K1, YO, slip 1, K1, PSSO; repeat from ★ across to last 5 sts, K1, (P1, K1) twice.

Row 14: K1, (P1, K1) twice, purl across to last 5 sts, K1, (P1, K1) twice.

Rows 15-26: Repeat Rows 9-14 twice.

Row 27: K1, (P1, K1) twice, K2 tog, YO, K1, YO, slip 1, K1, PSSO, K1, ★ (P1, K1) 3 times, K2 tog, YO, K1, YO, slip 1, K1, PSSO, K1; repeat from ★ across to last 4 sts, (P1, K1) twice.

Row 28: K1, (P1, K1) twice, P5, K1, ★ (P1, K1) 3 times, P5, K1; repeat from ★ across to last 4 sts, (P1, K1) twice.

Rows 29-32: Repeat Rows 27 and 28 twice.

Repeat Rows 9-32 for pattern until Afghan measures approximately 42" from cast on edge, ending by working Row 26.

Last 7 Rows: K1, (P1, K1) across.

Bind off all sts in pattern.

Design by Jean Lampe.

BRIGHT AND CHEERY

Brighten baby's room with this cheery coverlet. The sunny accent will coordinate with lots of crib linens, especially bedding in primary solids.

Finished Size: 31" x 42"

MATERIALS

Sport Weight Yarn:
21 ounces, (600 grams, 1,980 yards)
24" Circular knitting needle, size 6 (4.00 mm)
or size needed for gauge
Crochet hook for fringe

GAUGE: In pattern, 28 sts and 36 rows = 4"

AFGHAN

Cast on 227 sts.

Row 1 (Right side): P2, ★ [slip 1, K2, PSSO *(Fig. 11, page 78)*], P2; repeat from ★ across: 182 sts.

Row 2: K2, ★ P1, YO *(Fig. 4b, page 77)*, P1, K2; repeat from ★ across: 227 sts.

Row 3: P2, (K3, P2) across.

Row 4: K2, (P3, K2) across.

Rows 5-12: Repeat Rows 1-4 twice.

Row 13: (P2, slip 1, K2, PSSO) twice, ★ (K3, P1) twice, K1, P1; repeat from ★ across to last 17 sts, K3, P1, K3, (slip 1, K2, PSSO, P2) twice: 223 sts.

Row 14: K2, P1, YO, P1, K2, P1, YO, P4, K1, P3, K1, P1, K1, ★ (P3, K1) twice, P1, K1; repeat from ★ across to last 15 sts, P3, K1, P4, YO, P1, K2, P1, YO, P1, K2: 227 sts.

Row 15: P2, K3, P2, K5, P1, K1, P1, ★ (K3, P1) twice, K1, P1; repeat from ★ across to last 12 sts, K5, P2, K3, P2.

Row 16: K2, P3, K2, P5, K1, P1, K1, ★ (P3, K1) twice, P1, K1; repeat from ★ across to last 12 sts, P5, K2, P3, K2.

Row 17: (P2, slip 1, K2, PSSO) twice, (K1, P1) 3 times, ★ (K2, P1) twice, (K1, P1) twice; repeat from ★ across to last 11 sts, K1, (slip 1, K2, PSSO, P2) twice: 223 sts.

Row 18: K2, P1, YO, P1, K2, P1, YO, P2, K1, (P1, K1) twice, ★ (P2, K1) twice, (P1, K1) twice; repeat from ★ across to last 9 sts, P2, YO, P1, K2, P1, YO, P1, K2: 227 sts.

Rows 19 and 20: Repeat Rows 15 and 16.

Rows 21 and 22: Repeat Rows 13 and 14.

Row 23: P2, K3, P2, K6, P1, ★ K2, P1, (K1, P1) twice, K2, P1; repeat from ★ across to last 13 sts, K6, P2, K3, P2.

Row 24: K2, P3, K2, P6, K1, ★ P2, K1, (P1, K1) twice, P2, K1; repeat from ★ across to last 13 sts, P6, K2, P3, K2.

Repeat Rows 13-24 for pattern until Afghan measures approximately 41" from cast on edge, ending by working Row 16.

Last 12 Rows: Repeat Rows 1-4, 3 times.

Bind off all sts in pattern.

Holding six 18" lengths of yarn together, add fringe evenly across short edges of Afghan through Step 2 *(see Fringe, page 80)*.

Design by Shobha Govindan.

BABY BLOCKS

The playful pattern of blocks on this sweet throw is created using a circular knitting needle. Sport weight yarn makes it extra-snuggly.

Finished Size: 31" x 42"

MATERIALS
Sport Weight Yarn:
   14 ounces, (400 grams, 1,760 yards)
24" Circular knitting needle, size 6 (4.00 mm)
   or size needed for gauge
Crochet hook for fringe

GAUGE: In pattern, 28 sts and 42 rows = 5"

AFGHAN
Cast on 175 sts.

Row 1 (Right side)**:** Purl across.

Row 2: K1, ★ P1 tbl *(Fig. 3b, page 77)*, K1; repeat from ★ across.

Rows 3-8: Repeat Rows 1 and 2, 3 times.

Row 9: P7, ★ K1, YO *(Fig. 4a, page 77)*, K2 tog *(Fig. 5, page 78)*, K4, P7; repeat from ★ across.

Row 10: K1, (P1 tbl, K1) 3 times, ★ P7, K1, (P1 tbl, K1) 3 times; repeat from ★ across.

Row 11: P7, (K2, YO, K2 tog, K3, P7) across.

Row 12: K1, (P1 tbl, K1) 3 times, ★ P7, K1, (P1 tbl, K1) 3 times; repeat from ★ across.

Row 13: P7, (K3, YO, K2 tog, K2, P7) across.

Row 14: K1, (P1 tbl, K1) 3 times, ★ P7, K1, (P1 tbl, K1) 3 times; repeat from ★ across.

Row 15: P7, (K4, YO, K2 tog, K1, P7) across.

Row 16: K1, (P1 tbl, K1) 3 times, ★ P7, K1, (P1 tbl, K1) 3 times; repeat from ★ across.

Row 17: P7, (K5, YO, K2 tog, P7) across.

Row 18: K1, (P1 tbl, K1) 3 times, ★ P7, K1, (P1 tbl, K1) 3 times; repeat from ★ across.

Repeat Rows 3-18 for pattern until Afghan measures approximately 42" from cast on edge, ending by working Row 8.

Bind off all sts in **purl**.

Holding four 14" lengths of yarn together, add fringe evenly across short edges of Afghan through Step 1 *(see Fringe, page 80)*.

Design by Jean Lampe.

PRICELESS WHITE DIAMONDS

A precious pattern of diamonds gives this dazzling wrap a wealth of beauty. Over the years, its sentimental value will become priceless!

Finished Size: 32" x 42"

MATERIALS

Sport Weight Yarn:
 17 ounces, (480 grams, 1,605 yards)
24" Circular knitting needle, size 6 (4.00 mm)
 or size needed for gauge
Crochet hook for fringe

GAUGE: In pattern, 22 sts and 34 rows = 4"

AFGHAN

Cast on 175 sts.

Row 1 (Right side)**:** Purl across.

Row 2: Slip 1 as if to **knit**, ★ P1 tbl *(Fig. 3b, page 77)*, K1; repeat from ★ across.

Row 3: Slip 1 as if to **purl**, purl across.

Row 4: Slip 1 as if to **knit**, (P1 tbl, K1) across.

Rows 5-10: Repeat Rows 3 and 4, 3 times.

Row 11: Slip 1 as if to **purl**, P5, K1, ★ K2 tog *(Fig. 5, page 78)*, YO *(Fig. 4a, page 77)*, K1, YO, K2 tog tbl *(Fig. 6, page 78)*, K1; repeat from ★ across to last 6 sts, P6.

Row 12: Slip 1 as if to **knit**, P1 tbl, (K1, P1 tbl) twice, purl across to last 6 sts, (P1 tbl, K1) 3 times.

Row 13: Slip 1 as if to **purl**, P5, K2 tog, YO, K3, ★ YO, [slip, slip, K1, P2SSO *(Figs. 14a & b, page 79)*], YO, K3; repeat from ★ across to last 8 sts, YO, K2 tog tbl, P6.

Row 14: Slip 1 as if to **knit**, P1 tbl, (K1, P1 tbl) twice, purl across to last 6 sts, (P1 tbl, K1) 3 times.

Row 15: Slip 1 as if to **purl**, P5, K1, ★ YO, K2 tog tbl, K1, K2 tog, YO, K1; repeat from ★ across to last 6 sts, P6.

Row 16: Slip 1 as if to **knit**, P1 tbl, (K1, P1 tbl) twice, purl across to last 6 sts, (P1 tbl, K1) 3 times.

Row 17: Slip 1 as if to **purl**, P5, K2, YO, slip, slip, K1, P2SSO, ★ YO, K3, YO, slip, slip, K1, P2SSO; repeat from ★ across to last 8 sts, YO, K2, P6.

Row 18: Slip 1 as if to **knit**, P1 tbl, (K1, P1 tbl) twice, purl across to last 6 sts, (P1 tbl, K1) 3 times.

Repeat Rows 11-18 for pattern until Afghan measures approximately 41" from cast on edge, ending by working Row 18.

Last 10 Rows: Repeat Rows 3 and 4, 5 times.

Bind off all sts in pattern.

Holding seven 14" lengths of yarn together, add fringe evenly across short edges of Afghan through Step 1 *(see Fringe, page 80)*.

Design by Shobha Govindan.

HEIRLOOM BABY WRAP

An heirloom in the making, this elegant afghan has luxurious styling.
Alternating solid and openwork areas give the ornate throw classic detailing.

Finished Size: 34" x 42"

MATERIALS
Worsted Weight Yarn:
   21 ounces, (600 grams, 925 yards)
29" Circular knitting needle, size 10 (6.00 mm)
   or size needed for gauge
Cable needle

GAUGE: In Stockinette Stitch,
     16 sts and 20 rows = 4"

STITCH GUIDE

CABLE (uses 4 sts)
Slip next 2 sts onto cable needle and hold in **back** of work, K2 from left needle, K2 from cable needle.

AFGHAN
Cast on 135 sts.

Rows 1-9: Purl across.

Row 10 (Right side): P4, [slip 1, K1, PSSO *(Fig. 10, page 78)*], YO *(Fig. 4a, page 77)*, K3, YO, K2 tog *(Fig. 5, page 78)*, ★ P2, K4, P2, slip 1, K1, PSSO, YO, K3, YO, K2 tog; repeat from ★ across to last 4 sts, P4.

Row 11 AND ALL WRONG SIDE ROWS:
Purl across.

Row 12: P4, K2, YO, [slip 1, K2 tog, PSSO *(Figs. 12a & b, page 79)*], YO, K2, ★ P2, work Cable, P2, K2, YO, slip 1, K2 tog, PSSO, YO, K2; repeat from ★ across to last 4 sts, P4.

Row 14: P4, slip 1, K1, PSSO, YO, K3, YO, K2 tog, ★ P2, K4, P2, slip 1, K1, PSSO, YO, K3, YO, K2 tog; repeat from ★ across to last 4 sts, P4.

Row 16: P4, K2, YO, slip 1, K2 tog, PSSO, YO, K2, ★ P2, K4, P2, K2, YO, slip 1, K2 tog, PSSO, YO, K2; repeat from ★ across to last 4 sts, P4.

Row 18: P4, slip 1, K1, PSSO, YO, K3, YO, K2 tog, ★ P2, work Cable, P2, slip 1, K1, PSSO, YO, K3, YO, K2 tog; repeat from ★ across to last 4 sts, P4.

Row 20: P4, K2, YO, slip 1, K2 tog, PSSO, YO, K2, ★ P2, K4, P2, K2, YO, slip 1, K2 tog, PSSO, YO, K2; repeat from ★ across to last 4 sts, P4.

Row 21: Purl across.

Row 22: P4, slip 1, K1, PSSO, YO, K3, YO, K2 tog, ★ P2, K4, P2, slip 1, K1, PSSO, YO, K3, YO, K2 tog; repeat from ★ across to last 4 sts, P4.

Repeat Rows 11-22 for pattern until Afghan measures approximately 41" from cast on edge, ending by working Row 20.

Last 8 Rows: Purl across.

Bind off all sts in **purl**.

Design by Rachel J. Terrill.

A reflection of sunny spring days, this captivating little cover-up has alternating columns of cables and crowns. What a bright and charming accessory for the nursery!

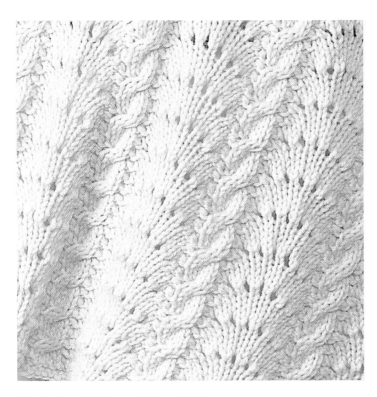

Finished Size: 37" x 47"

MATERIALS

Worsted Weight Yarn:
    20 ounces, (570 grams, 1,315 yards)
29" Circular knitting needle, size 9 (5.50 mm)
    or size needed for gauge
Cable needle

GAUGE: In pattern, 19 sts and 22 rows = 4"

STITCH GUIDE

CABLE (uses 4 sts)
Slip next 2 sts onto cable needle and hold in **back** of work, K2 from left needle, K2 from cable needle.

AFGHAN

Cast on 178 sts.

Rows 1-3: Knit across.

Row 4 (Right side)**:** K9, P2 tog *(Fig. 8, page 78)*, K4, P2 tog, ★ K 11, P2 tog, K4, P2 tog; repeat from ★ across to last 9 sts, K9: 160 sts.

Row 5: K3, purl across to last 3 sts, K3.

Row 6: K8, P2 tog, K4, P2 tog, ★ K9, P2 tog, K4, P2 tog; repeat from ★ across to last 8 sts, K8: 142 sts.

Row 7: K3, purl across to last 3 sts, K3.

Row 8: K4, **[**YO *(Fig. 4a, page 77)*, K1**]** 3 times, P2 tog, work Cable, P2 tog, ★ K1, (YO, K1) 6 times, P2 tog, work Cable, P2 tog; repeat from ★ across to last 7 sts, (K1, YO) 3 times, K4: 178 sts.

Row 9: K3, purl across to last 3 sts, K3.

Repeat Rows 4-9 for pattern until Afghan measures approximately 46" from cast on edge, ending by working Row 9.

Last 4 Rows: Knit across.

Bind off all sts in **knit**.

Design by Carole Prior.

BLUE TRANQUILLITY

Traditionally associated with baby boys, the color blue elicits peace and tranquillity.
What better way to get your rough-and-tumble tot to sleep than with this restful wrap!

Finished Size: 34" x 42"

MATERIALS
Worsted Weight Yarn:
23 ounces, (650 grams, 1,010 yards)
29" Circular knitting needle, size 10 (6.00 mm)
or size needed for gauge

GAUGE: In Stockinette Stitch,
16 sts and 20 rows = 4"

AFGHAN
Cast on 135 sts.

Rows 1-7: Knit across.

Row 8 (Right side)**:** K9, K2 tog *(Fig. 5, page 78)*, ★ YO *(Fig. 4a, page 77)*, K3, K2 tog; repeat from ★ across to last 9 sts, YO, K9.

Row 9: K9, P2, (K3, P2) across to last 9 sts, K9.

Row 10: K8, K2 tog, (YO, K3, K2 tog) across to last 5 sts, YO, K5.

Row 11: K5, P2, (K3, P2) across to last 8 sts, K8.

Row 12: K7, K2 tog, (YO, K3, K2 tog) across to last 6 sts, YO, K6.

Row 13: K6, P2, (K3, P2) across to last 7 sts, K7.

Row 14: K6, K2 tog, (YO, K3, K2 tog) across to last 7 sts, YO, K7.

Row 15: K7, P2, (K3, P2) across to last 6 sts, K6.

Row 16: K5, K2 tog, (YO, K3, K2 tog) across to last 8 sts, YO, K8.

Row 17: K8, P2, (K3, P2) across to last 5 sts, K5.

Row 18: K4, K2 tog, (YO, K3, K2 tog) across to last 4 sts, YO, K4.

Row 19: K4, P2, (K3, P2) across to last 4 sts, K4.

Repeat Rows 10-19 for pattern until Afghan measures approximately 41" from cast on edge, ending by working Row 17.

Next Row: K4, K2 tog, (YO, K3, K2 tog) across to last 9 sts, YO, K9.

Next Row: K9, P2, (K3, P2) across to last 4 sts, K4.

Last 8 Rows: Knit across.

Bind off all sts in **knit**.

Design by Rachel J. Terrill.

LULLABY

Your little doll is sure to have pleasant dreams cradled in this elegant pink afghan. It's as pretty as a lullaby and just as sweet!

Finished Size: 35" x 43"

MATERIALS
Worsted Weight Yarn:
22$^1/_2$ ounces, (640 grams, 1,310 yards)
29" Circular knitting needle, size 7 (4.50 mm)
or size needed for gauge

GAUGE: In pattern, 30 sts and 39 rows = 6"

AFGHAN
Cast on 176 sts.

Rows 1 and 2: Purl across.

Row 3 (Right side)**:** P5, K1, YO *(Fig. 4a, page 77)*, K1, P4, P2 tog twice *(Fig. 8, page 78)*, P4, K1, ★ (YO, K1) twice, P4, P2 tog twice, P4, K1; repeat from ★ across to last 6 sts, YO, K1, P5.

Row 4: Purl across.

Row 5: P5, K1, ★ YO, K2, P3, P2 tog twice, P3, K2, YO, K1; repeat from ★ across to last 5 sts, P5.

Row 6: Purl across.

Row 7: P5, K1, ★ YO, K3, P2, P2 tog twice, P2, K3, YO, K1; repeat from ★ across to last 5 sts, P5.

Row 8: Purl across.

Row 9: P5, K1, ★ YO, K4, P1, P2 tog twice, P1, K4, YO, K1; repeat from ★ across to last 5 sts, P5.

Row 10: Purl across.

Row 11: P5, K1, ★ YO, K5, P2 tog twice, K5, YO, K1; repeat from ★ across to last 5 sts, P5.

Row 12: Purl across.

Row 13: P5, K1, YO, K1, P4, P2 tog twice, P4, K1, ★ (YO, K1) twice, P4, P2 tog twice, P4, K1; repeat from ★ across to last 6 sts, YO, K1, P5.

Repeat Rows 4-13 for pattern until Afghan measures approximately 42" from cast on edge, ending by working Row 11.

Last 2 Rows: Purl across.

Bind off all sts in **knit**.

Design by Rachel J. Terrill.

DECKED IN DIAMONDS

Decked in decorative diamonds, this jewel of a throw will wrap your precious bundle of joy in rich softness.

Finished Size: 34" x 48"

MATERIALS
Worsted Weight Yarn:
   17 ounces, (480 grams, 1,120 yards)
   29" Circular knitting needle, size 9 (5.50 mm)
   or size needed for gauge

GAUGE: In pattern, 16 sts and 24 rows = 4"

AFGHAN
Cast on 137 sts.

Rows 1-5: Knit across.

Row 6 (Right side)**:** K7, K2 tog *(Fig. 5, page 78)*, YO *(Fig. 4a, page 77)*, K8, ★ K2 tog, YO, K8; repeat from ★ across.

Row 7: K3, purl across to last 3 sts, K3.

Row 8: K6, K2 tog, YO, K1, YO, [slip 1, K1, PSSO *(Fig. 10, page 78)*], ★ K5, K2 tog, YO, K1, YO, slip 1, K1, PSSO; repeat from ★ across to last 6 sts, K6.

Row 9: K3, purl across to last 3 sts, K3.

Row 10: K5, K2 tog, YO, K3, YO, slip 1, K1, PSSO, ★ K3, K2 tog, YO, K3, YO, slip 1, K1, PSSO; repeat from ★ across to last 5 sts, K5.

Row 11: K3, purl across to last 3 sts, K3.

Row 12: K4, K2 tog, YO, K1, YO, [slip 1, K2 tog, PSSO *(Figs. 12a & b, page 79)*], YO, K1, YO, slip 1, K1, PSSO, ★ K1, K2 tog, YO, K1, YO, slip 1, K2 tog, PSSO, YO, K1, YO, slip 1, K1, PSSO; repeat from ★ across to last 4 sts, K4.

Row 13: K3, purl across to last 3 sts, K3.

Row 14: K3, K2 tog, YO, K7, ★ YO, slip 1, K2 tog, PSSO, YO, K7; repeat from ★ across to last 5 sts, YO, slip 1, K1, PSSO, K3.

Row 15: K3, purl across to last 3 sts, K3.

Row 16: K5, YO, slip 1, K2 tog, PSSO, YO, K1, YO, slip 1, K2 tog, PSSO, ★ YO, K3, YO, slip 1, K2 tog, PSSO, YO, K1, YO, slip 1, K2 tog, PSSO; repeat from ★ across to last 5 sts, YO, K5.

Row 17: K3, purl across to last 3 sts, K3.

Row 18: K5, K2 tog, YO, K3, YO, slip 1, K1, PSSO, ★ K3, K2 tog, YO, K3, YO, slip 1, K1, PSSO; repeat from ★ across to last 5 sts, K5.

Row 19: K3, purl across to last 3 sts, K3.

Row 20: K7, ★ YO, slip 1, K2 tog, PSSO, YO, K7; repeat from ★ across.

Row 21: K3, purl across to last 3 sts, K3.

Repeat Rows 6-21 for pattern until Afghan measures approximately 47" from cast on edge, ending by working Row 7.

Last 5 Rows: Knit across.

Bind off all sts in **knit**.

Design by Carole Prior.

SLEEPYTIME SEASHELLS

Rows of shells give seashore styling to this cover-up, which is awash in a shade of blue reminiscent of coastal waters. What a great companion for an outing at the beach!

Finished Size: 34" x 45"

MATERIALS

Worsted Weight Yarn:
  20 ounces, (570 grams, 1,315 yards)
  29" Circular knitting needle, size 9 (5.50 mm)
  or size needed for gauge

GAUGE: In pattern, 16 sts and 24 rows = 4"

STITCH GUIDE

KNIT 4 TOGETHER
(abbreviated K4 tog)
Insert the right needle into the **front** of the first 4 stitches on the left needle as if to **knit** **(Fig. A)**, then knit them together.

Fig. A

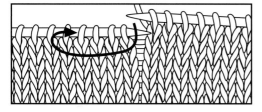

KNIT 4 TOGETHER THROUGH BACK LOOP *(abbreviated K4 tog tbl)*
Insert the right needle into the **back** of the first 4 stitches on the left needle from **front** to **back** *(Fig. B)*, then knit them together.

Fig. B

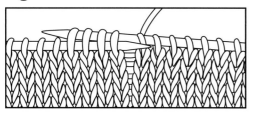

AFGHAN

Cast on 135 sts.

Rows 1-5: Knit across.

Row 6 (Right side)**:** K5, YO **(Fig. 4a, page 77)**, K8, ★ YO, K1, YO, K8; repeat from ★ across to last 5 sts, YO, K5: 163 sts.

Row 7: K6, P8, (K3, P8) across to last 6 sts, K6.

Row 8: K6, YO, K8, ★ YO, K3, YO K8; repeat from ★ across to last 6 sts, YO, K6: 191 sts.

Row 9: K7, P8, (K5, P8) across to last 7 sts, K7.

Row 10: K7, YO, K8, ★ YO, K5, YO, K8; repeat from ★ across to last 7 sts, YO, K7: 219 sts.

Row 11: K8, P8, (K7, P8) across to last 8 sts, K8.

Row 12: K8, K4 tog tbl, K4 tog, ★ K7, K4 tog tbl, K4 tog; repeat from ★ across to last 8 sts, K8: 135 sts.

Row 13: Knit across.

Repeat Rows 6-13 for pattern until Afghan measures approximately 44" from cast on edge, ending by working Row 13.

Last 5 Rows: Knit across.

Bind off all sts in **knit**.

Design by Carole Prior.

BABY'S FIRST BUILDING BLOCKS

*As you begin building your baby's collection of cuddly cover-ups,
be sure to include this eye-catching throw of blue-edged blocks.*

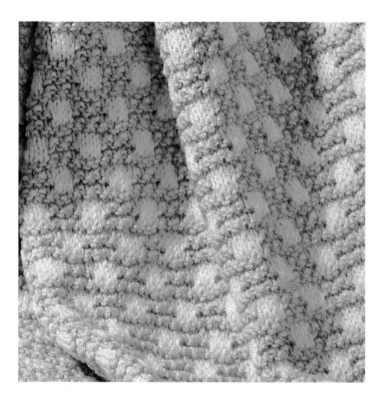

Finished Size: 29" x 42"

MATERIALS
Worsted Weight Yarn:
   Blue - 14 ounces, (400 grams, 815 yards)
   White - 9 ounces, (260 grams, 525 yards)
   29" Circular knitting needles, sizes 9 (5.50 mm)
   and 10 (6.00 mm) **or** sizes needed for gauge

GAUGE: With larger size needle, in pattern,
         21 sts = 4$^1/_4$" and 40 rows = 4$^1/_2$"

AFGHAN
With smaller size needle and Blue, cast on 141 sts.

Rows 1-7: Knit across.

When instructed to slip a stitch, always slip as if to **purl** with yarn to **wrong** side.

Change to larger size needle.

Row 8 (Right side)**:** K5, with White, (K1, slip 1) twice, K3, ★ slip 1, (K1, slip 1) twice, K3; repeat from ★ across to last 9 sts, (slip 1, K1) twice, with second Blue, K5 *(Fig. 15, page 79)*.

Row 9: K5, with White, (K1, slip 1) twice, P3, ★ slip 1, (K1, slip 1) twice, P3; repeat from ★ across to last 9 sts, (slip 1, K1) twice, with second Blue, K5.

Rows 10 and 11: With Blue, K9, slip 3, (K5, slip 3) across to last 9 sts, K9.

Rows 12 and 13: Repeat Rows 8 and 9.

Rows 14 and 15: With Blue, knit across.

Row 16: K5, with White, K3, ★ slip 1, (K1, slip 1) twice, K3; repeat from ★ across to last 5 sts, with second Blue, K5.

Row 17: K5, with White, P3, ★ slip 1, (K1, slip 1) twice, P3; repeat from ★ across to last 5 sts, with second Blue, K5.

Rows 18 and 19: With Blue, K5, (slip 3, K5) across.

Rows 20 and 21: Repeat Rows 16 and 17.

Rows 22 and 23: With Blue, knit across.

Repeat Rows 8-23 for pattern until Afghan measures approximately 41" from cast on edge, ending by working Row 13.

Change to smaller size needle.

Last 6 Rows: With Blue, knit across.

Bind off all sts in **knit**.

Design by Rachel J. Terrill.

ROCK-A-BYE WRAP

Knitted with pretty pastel yarn and finished with a lacy edging, our sweet afghan is as soft as Baby's skin. What a snuggly way to drift off to Dreamland!

Finished Size: 38" x 38"

MATERIALS

Fingering Weight Yarn:

White - 6 ounces, (170 grams, 860 yards)

Green - 4 ounces, (110 grams, 575 yards)

Pink - 4 ounces, (110 grams, 575 yards)

29" Circular **and** 10" straight knitting needles, size 8 (5.00 mm) **or** size needed for gauge

GAUGE: In pattern, 24 sts and 24 rows = 4"

AFGHAN BODY

With White, cast on 199 sts.

Row 1: Purl across; drop White.

When instructed to slip a stitch throughout Afghan Body, always slip as if to **purl** with yarn to **wrong** side.

Row 2 (Right side)**:** With Green, K3, (slip 1, K3) across.

Row 3: K3, (slip 1, K3) across; drop Green.

Row 4: With White, K1, slip 1, (K3, slip 1) across to last st, K1.

Row 5: P1, slip 1, (P3, slip 1) across to last st, P1; drop White.

Rows 6 and 7: With Pink, repeat Rows 2 and 3; at end of Row 7, drop Pink.

Rows 8 and 9: Repeat Rows 4 and 5.

Repeat Rows 2-9 for pattern until Afghan Body measures approximately 33" from cast on edge, ending by working Row 7.

Cut Green and Pink.

With White, bind off all sts in **knit**.

EDGING

With White, cast on 8 sts.

Row 1: K6, increase *(see Increases, page 77)*, WYF slip 1 as if to **purl**: 9 sts.

Row 2 (Right side)**:** K1 tbl *(Fig. 3a, page 77)*, K1, ★ YO *(Fig. 4a, page 77)*, [slip 1 as if to **knit**, K1, PSSO *(Fig. 10, page 78)*], K1; repeat from ★ once **more**, WYF slip 1 as if to **purl**.

Note: Loop a short piece of yarn around any stitch to mark Row 2 as **right** side.

Row 3: K1 tbl, K7, increase, **turn**; cast on 2 sts: 12 sts.

Row 4: K1, increase, K2, ★ YO, slip 1 as if to **knit**, K1, PSSO, K1; repeat from ★ once **more**, YO, K1, WYF slip 1 as if to **purl**: 14 sts.

Row 5: K1 tbl, K 11, increase, WYF slip 1 as if to **purl**: 15 sts.

Row 6: K1 tbl, increase, K2, YO, slip 1 as if to **knit**, K1, PSSO, ★ K1, YO, slip 1 as if to **knit**, K1, PSSO; repeat from ★ once **more**, K2, WYF slip 1 as if to **purl**: 16 sts.

Row 7: K1 tbl, K 13, K2 tog *(Fig. 5, page 78)*: 15 sts.

Row 8: Slip 1 as if to **purl**, K1, PSSO, slip 1 as if to **knit**, K1, PSSO, K4, ★ YO, slip 1 as if to **knit**, K1, PSSO, K1; repeat from ★ once **more**, WYF slip 1 as if to **purl**: 13 sts.

Row 9: K1 tbl, K 10, K2 tog: 12 sts.

Row 10: Bind off 3 sts, K2, YO, slip 1 as if to **knit**, K1, PSSO, K1, YO, slip 1 as if to **knit**, K1, PSSO, WYF slip 1 as if to **purl**: 9 sts.

Repeat Rows 3-10 until Edging is long enough to fit around Afghan Body when slightly stretched plus 16 rows (2 points) for every corner, ending by working Row 10.

Bind off all sts in **knit**.

FINISHING

Sew ends together then sew straight edge of Edging to Afghan Body, pleating 16 rows at each corner.

Design by Tricia Gardella.

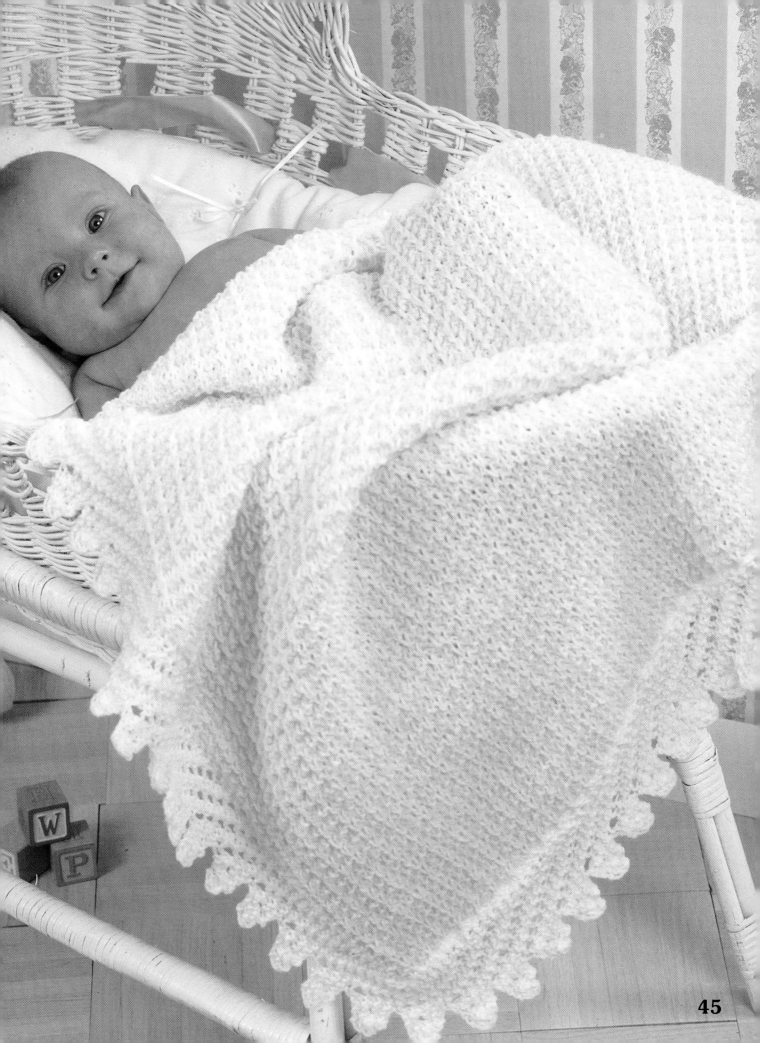

PATCHWORK PLEASER

Your precious bundle will make an impressive presentation draped in this lovely patchwork-look afghan with tied "quilt" squares!

Finished Size: 37" x 45"

MATERIALS

Worsted Weight Yarn:
  16 ounces, (450 grams, 1,040 yards)
29" Circular knitting needle, size 11 (8.00 mm)
  or size needed for gauge
Markers
Yarn needle

GAUGE: In Stockinette Stitch,
     14 sts and 18 rows = 4"

See Yarn Overs and Decreases, pages 77-79, before beginning.

AFGHAN

Cast on 116 sts.

Rows 1-6: Knit across.

Row 7 (Right side)**:** K4, place marker *(see Markers, page 76)*, K 12, place marker, ★ (YO, K2 tog) 6 times, place marker, K 12, place marker; repeat from ★ 3 times **more**, K4.

Row 8: K4, P 12, ★ (YO, P2 tog) 6 times, P 12; repeat from ★ 3 times **more**, K4.

Rows 9-22: Repeat Rows 7 and 8, 7 times.

Row 23: K4, (YO, K2 tog) 6 times, ★ K 12, (YO, K2 tog) 6 times; repeat from ★ 3 times **more**, K4.

Row 24: K4, (YO, P2 tog) 6 times, ★ P 12, (YO, P2 tog) 6 times; repeat from ★ 3 times **more**, K4.

Rows 25-38: Repeat Rows 23 and 24, 7 times.

Repeat Rows 7-38 for pattern until Afghan measures approximately 44" from cast on edge, ending by working Row 38.

Last 6 Rows: Knit across.

Bind off all sts in **knit**.

FINISHING

Thread yarn needle with two 10" lengths of yarn. With **right** side of Afghan facing, insert needle around center st of each solid square and draw yarn through. Tie knot and trim ends to desired length.

Design by John Feddersen, Jr.

WINTRY WARMER

Our wonderful white wrap will keep your baby warm all winter long! Covered with a classic diamond pattern, this comforter reflects just how precious your baby is to you.

Finished Size: 31" x 42"

MATERIALS
Worsted Weight Yarn:
    17 ounces, (480 grams, 990 yards)
29" Circular knitting needle, size 10 (6.00 mm)
    or size needed for gauge

GAUGE: In Stockinette Stitch,
    16 sts and 20 rows = 4"

STITCH GUIDE

> **RIGHT TWIST** *(abbreviated RT)*
> (uses 2 sts)
> K2 tog but do **not** slip sts off needle, knit first st again, slipping both sts off left needle.

AFGHAN

Cast on 135 sts.

Rows 1-7: K1, (P1, K1) across.

Row 8 (Increase row): (K1, P1) twice, increase *(see Increases, page 77)*, (P1, K1) across: 136 sts.

Row 9: (K1, P1) twice, K3, P3, ★ K2, P 10, K2, P3; repeat from ★ across to last 7 sts, K3, (P1, K1) twice.

Row 10 (Right side): K1, (P1, K1) twice, P2, [slip 1, K2, PSSO *(Fig. 11, page 78)*], P2, ★ K2, K2 tog *(Fig. 5, page 78)*, YO *(Fig. 4a, page 77)*, RT, YO, SSK *(Figs. 13a-c, page 79)*, K2, P2, slip 1, K2, PSSO, P2; repeat from ★ across to last 5 sts, K1, (P1, K1) twice: 128 sts.

Row 11: (K1, P1) twice, K3, P2, ★ K2, P 10, K2, P2; repeat from ★ across to last 7 sts, K3, (P1, K1) twice.

Row 12: K1, (P1, K1) twice, P2, K1, YO, K1, P2, ★ K1, K2 tog, YO, K4, YO, SSK, K1, P2, K1, YO, K1, P2; repeat from ★ across to last 5 sts, K1, (P1, K1) twice: 136 sts.

Row 13: (K1, P1) twice, K3, P3, ★ K2, P 10, K2, P3; repeat from ★ across to last 7 sts, K3, (P1, K1) twice.

Row 14: K1, (P1, K1) twice, P2, slip 1, K2, PSSO, P2, ★ K2 tog, YO, K1, K2 tog, YO twice, SSK, K1, YO, SSK, P2, slip 1, K2, PSSO, P2; repeat from ★ across to last 5 sts, K1, (P1, K1) twice: 128 sts.

Row 15: (K1, P1) twice, K3, P2, ★ K2, P4, K1, P5, K2, P2; repeat from ★ across to last 7 sts, K3, (P1, K1) twice.

Row 16: K1, (P1, K1) twice, P2, K1, YO, K1, P2, ★ K2, YO, SSK, K2, K2 tog, YO, K2, P2, K1, YO, K1, P2; repeat from ★ across to last 5 sts, K1, (P1, K1) twice: 136 sts.

Row 17: (K1, P1) twice, K3, P3, ★ K2, P 10, K2, P3; repeat from ★ across to last 7 sts, K3, (P1, K1) twice.

Row 18: K1, (P1, K1) twice, P2, slip 1, K2, PSSO, P2, ★ K3, YO, SSK, K2 tog, YO, K3, P2, slip 1, K2, PSSO, P2; repeat from ★ across to last 5 sts, K1, (P1, K1) twice: 128 sts.

Row 19: (K1, P1) twice, K3, P2, ★ K2, P 10, K2, P2; repeat from ★ across to last 7 sts, K3, (P1, K1) twice.

Row 20: K1, (P1, K1) twice, P2, K1, YO, K1, P2, ★ K2, K2 tog, YO, RT, YO, SSK, K2, P2, K1, YO, K1, P2; repeat from ★ across to last 5 sts, K1, (P1, K1) twice: 136 sts.

Row 21: (K1, P1) twice, K3, P3, ★ K2, P 10, K2, P3; repeat from ★ across to last 7 sts, K3, (P1, K1) twice.

Continued on page 72.

LITTLE BOY BLUE

Your Little Boy Blue is sure to blow his horn over this simply charming afghan! You will too, when you see how fun and easy it is to make.

Finished Size: 33" x 44"

MATERIALS
Worsted Weight Yarn:
    19 ounces, (540 grams, 1,110 yards)
    29" Circular knitting needles, sizes 9 (5.50 mm)
    and 10 (6.00 mm) **or** sizes needed for gauge

GAUGE: With larger size needle,
    in Stockinette Stitch,
    16 sts and 20 rows = 4"

AFGHAN

With smaller size needle, cast on 134 sts.

Rows 1-7: Knit across.

Change to larger size needle.

Row 8 (Right side)**:** Knit across.

Row 9: K5, purl across to last 5 sts, K5.

Rows 10 and 11: Repeat Rows 8 and 9.

Row 12: K 18, YO (*Fig. 4a, page 77*), SSK (*Figs. 13a-c, page 79*), (K 14, YO, SSK) across to last 18 sts, K 18.

Row 13: K5, purl across to last 5 sts, K5.

Row 14: K 17, (YO, SSK) twice, ★ K 12, (YO, SSK) twice; repeat from ★ across to last 17 sts, K 17.

Row 15: K5, purl across to last 5 sts, K5.

Row 16: K 16, (YO, SSK) 3 times, ★ K 10, (YO, SSK) 3 times; repeat from ★ across to last 16 sts, K 16.

Row 17: K5, purl across to last 5 sts, K5.

Row 18: K 17, (YO, SSK) twice, ★ K 12, (YO, SSK) twice; repeat from ★ across to last 17 sts, K 17.

Row 19: K5, purl across to last 5 sts, K5.

Row 20: K 18, YO, SSK, (K 14, YO, SSK) across to last 18 sts, K 18.

Row 21: K5, purl across to last 5 sts, K5.

Row 22: Knit across.

Rows 23-25: Repeat Rows 21 and 22 once, then repeat Row 21 once **more**.

Row 26: K 10, YO, SSK, (K 14, YO, SSK) across to last 10 sts, K 10.

Row 27: K5, purl across to last 5 sts, K5.

Row 28: K9, (YO, SSK) twice, ★ K 12, (YO, SSK) twice; repeat from ★ across to last 9 sts, K9.

Row 29: K5, purl across to last 5 sts, K5.

Row 30: K8, (YO, SSK) 3 times, ★ K 10, (YO, SSK) 3 times; repeat from ★ across to last 8 sts, K8.

Row 31: K5, purl across to last 5 sts, K5.

Row 32: K9, (YO, SSK) twice, ★ K 12, (YO, SSK) twice; repeat from ★ across to last 9 sts, K9.

Row 33: K5, purl across to last 5 sts, K5.

Row 34: K 10, YO, SSK, (K 14, YO, SSK) across to last 10 sts, K 10.

Rows 35-39: Repeat Rows 21 and 22 twice, then repeat Row 21 once **more**.

Row 40: K 18, YO, SSK, (K 14, YO, SSK) across to last 18 sts, K 18.

Repeat Rows 13-40 for pattern until Afghan measures approximately $42^1/_2$" from cast on edge, ending by working Row 24.

Change to smaller size needle.

Last 6 Rows: Knit across.

Bind off all sts in **knit**.

Design by Rachel J. Terrill.

BASKET WEAVE BLANKET

Featuring a classic basket weave pattern that's worked in aran, this versatile throw is a perfect take-a-long for any occasion.

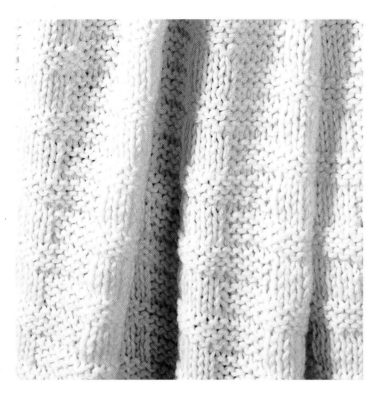

Finished Size: 36" x 45"

MATERIALS

Worsted Weight Yarn:
 18 ounces, (510 grams, 1,175 yards)
 29" Circular knitting needle, size 11 (8.00 mm)
 or size needed for gauge

GAUGE: In pattern, 14 sts and 20 rows = 4"

AFGHAN

Cast on 127 sts.

Rows 1-10: Knit across.

Row 11: K 11, P5, (K 15, P5) across to last 11 sts, K 11.

Row 12: K6, P5, K5, (P 15, K5) across to last 11 sts, P5, K6.

Row 13: K 11, P5, (K 15, P5) across to last 11 sts, K 11.

Row 14: Knit across.

Row 15: K6, (K 15, P5) across to last 21 sts, K 21.

Row 16: K6, P 15, (K5, P 15) across to last 6 sts, K6.

Row 17: K6, (K 15, P5) across to last 21 sts, K 21.

Row 18: Knit across.

Repeat Rows 11-18 for pattern until Afghan measures approximately 43" from cast on edge, ending by working Row 14.

Last 10 Rows: Knit across.

Bind off all sts in **knit**.

Design by John Feddersen, Jr.

Sweet dreams are only moments away when your child slumbers under this playful throw. Knitted in soothing colors, this afghan will work for boys as well as girls!

Finished Size: 32" x 41"

MATERIALS

Worsted Weight Yarn:
  White - 12 ounces, (340 grams, 780 yards)
  Yellow - 4 ounces, (110 grams, 260 yards)
  Green - 4 ounces, (110 grams, 260 yards)
29" Circular knitting needle, size 9 (5.50 mm)
  or size needed for gauge
Crochet hook, size H (5.50 mm) for Trim

GAUGE: In pattern, 22 sts = 4¹/₂";
              28 rows = 4¹/₄"

STITCH GUIDE

JOINING WITH SC

When instructed to join with sc, begin with a slip knot on hook. Insert hook in st indicated, YO and pull up a loop, YO and draw through both loops on hook *(Figs. A & B)*.

Fig. A

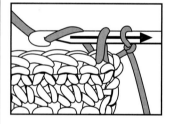

Fig. B

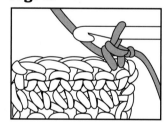

SINGLE CROCHET

Insert hook in st indicated, YO and pull up a loop, YO and draw through both loops on hook *(Fig. C)*.

Fig. C

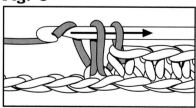

AFGHAN BODY

With White, cast on 154 sts.

Rows 1-5: Knit across.

Carry the White **loosely** along the edge, cutting other colors as indicated.

Row 6 (Right side)**:** Drop White; with Yellow, ★ K2 tog *(Fig. 5, page 78)*, K2, increase twice *(see Increases, page 77)*, K3, SSK *(Figs. 13a-c, page 79)*; repeat from ★ across.

Row 7: Purl across.

Row 8: ★ K2 tog, K2, increase twice, K3, SSK; repeat from ★ across.

Rows 9-11: Repeat Rows 7 and 8 once, then repeat Row 7 once **more**.

Row 12: Cut Yellow; with White, ★ K2 tog, K2, increase twice, K3, SSK; repeat from ★ across.

Rows 13-17: Knit across.

Row 18: Drop White; with Green, ★ K2 tog, K2, increase twice, K3, SSK; repeat from ★ across.

Rows 19-23: Repeat Rows 7 and 8 twice, then repeat Row 7 once **more**.

Row 24: Cut Green; with White, ★ K2 tog, K2, increase twice, K3, SSK; repeat from ★ across.

Rows 25-29: Knit across.

Row 30: Drop White; with Yellow, ★ K2 tog, K2, increase twice, K3, SSK; repeat from ★ across.

Repeat Rows 7-30 for pattern until Afghan measures approximately 41" from cast on edge, ending by working Row 12.

Last 4 Rows: Knit across.

Bind off all sts in **knit**.

Continued on page 73.

As you wrap your little rose in the soft folds of this pretty fan and feather pattern creation, her natural beauty will bloom for all to see!

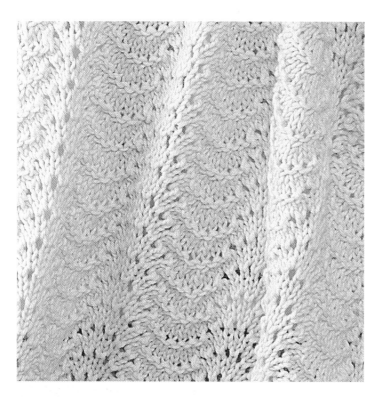

Finished Size: 35" x 45"

MATERIALS

Worsted Weight Yarn:
  20 ounces, (570 grams, 1,305 yards)
29" Circular knitting needle, size 11 (8.00 mm)
  or size needed for gauge

GAUGE: In Stockinette Stitch,
        14 sts and 18 rows = 4"

AFGHAN

Cast on 138 sts.

Rows 1-6: Knit across.

Row 7 (Wrong side)**:** K6, K2 tog 3 times *(Fig. 5, page 78)*, **[**YO *(Fig. 4a, page 77)*, K1**]** 6 times, ★ K2 tog 6 times, (YO, K1) 6 times; repeat from ★ across to last 12 sts, K2 tog 3 times, K6.

Row 8: Knit across.

Row 9: K6, purl across to last 6 sts, K6.

Row 10: Knit across.

Row 11: K6, K2 tog 3 times, (YO, K1) 6 times, ★ K2 tog 6 times, (YO, K1) 6 times; repeat from ★ across to last 12 sts, K2 tog 3 times, K6.

Repeat Rows 8-11 for pattern until Afghan measures approximately 44" from cast on edge, ending by working Row 10.

Last 6 Rows: Knit across.

Bind off all sts in **knit**.

Design by John Feddersen, Jr.

FOR A BONNY BABE

Your bonny babe's charm and personality will shine against the backdrop of this classic Irish knit afghan!

Finished Size: 26" x 32"

MATERIALS
Sport Weight Yarn:
   8 ounces, (230 grams, 870 yards)
29" Circular knitting needle, size 5 (3.75 mm)
   or size needed for gauge
Markers
Cable needle

GAUGE: In pattern, 22 sts and 32 rows = 4"

STITCH GUIDE

CABLE 2 BACK *(abbreviated C2B)*
   (uses 2 sts)
Slip next st onto cable needle and hold in **back** of work, K1 from left needle, K1 from cable needle.

CABLE 2 FRONT *(abbreviated C2F)*
   (uses 2 sts)
Slip next st onto cable needle and hold in **front** of work, K1 from left needle, K1 from cable needle.

CABLE 4 BACK *(abbreviated C4B)*
   (uses 4 sts)
Slip next 2 sts onto cable needle and hold in **back** of work, K2 from left needle, K2 from cable needle.

TWIST 2 BACK *(abbreviated T2B)*
   (uses 2 sts)
Slip next st onto cable needle and hold in **back** of work, K1 from left needle, P1 from cable needle.

TWIST 2 FRONT *(abbreviated T2F)*
   (uses 2 sts)
Slip next st onto cable needle and hold in **front** of work, P1 from left needle, K1 from cable needle.

PATTERN STITCHES

SMALL CABLE (uses 10 sts)
Row 1: K1, P2, C4B, P2, K1.
Row 2: P1, K2, P4, K2, P1.
Row 3: K1, P2, K4, P2, K1.
Row 4: P1, K2, P4, K2, P1.
Row 5: K1, P2, K4, P2, K1.
Row 6: P1, K2, P4, K2, P1.
Repeat Rows 1-6 for pattern.

CABLED DIAMOND (uses 12 sts)
Row 1: P4, C4B, P4.
Row 2: K4, P4, K4.
Row 3: P4, K4, P4.
Row 4: K4, P4, K4.
Row 5: P4, K4, P4.
Row 6: K4, P4, K4.
Row 7: P4, C4B, P4.
Row 8: K4, P4, K4.
Row 9: P4, K4, P4.
Row 10: K4, P4, K4.
Row 11: P4, C2B, T2F, P4.
Row 12: K4, P2, K1, P1, K4.
Row 13: P3, T2B, K1, P1, C2F, P3.
Row 14: K3, (P1, K1) twice, P2, K3.
Row 15: P2, C2B, (P1, K1) twice, T2F, P2.
Row 16: K2, P2, (K1, P1) 3 times, K2.
Row 17: P2, K2, (P1, K1) 3 times, P2.
Row 18: K2, P2, (K1, P1) 3 times, K2.
Row 19: P2, T2F, (P1, K1) twice, T2B, P2.
Row 20: K3, (P1, K1) twice, P2, K3.
Row 21: P3, T2F, K1, P1, T2B, P3.
Row 22: K4, P2, K1, P1, K4.
Row 23: P4, C2F, C2B, P4.
Row 24: K4, P4, K4.
Repeat Rows 1-24 for pattern.

AFGHAN
Cast on 139 sts.

Rows 1-16: K1, (P1, K1) across.

Continued on page 73.

PRETTY POSIES

*You'll enjoy the garden-fresh beauty of this floral afghan. Sprinkled
with pretty posies, it provides a perfect place for Baby to slumber.*

Finished Size: 36" x 42"

MATERIALS
Worsted Weight Yarn:
   White - 20 ounces, (570 grams, 1,315 yards)
   Green - 58 yards
   Blue - 39 yards
   Pink - 35 yards
   Yellow - 29 yards
   Lavender - 28 yards
29" Circular knitting needle, size 8 (5.00 mm)
   or size needed for gauge
Markers
Yarn needle

GAUGE: In Stockinette Stitch,
         18 sts and 24 rows = 4"

AFGHAN
With White, cast on 161 sts.

Rows 1-13: K1, (P1, K1) across.

Row 14 (Right side)**:** K1, (P1, K1) 4 times, place marker **(see Markers, page 76)**, knit across to last 9 sts, place marker, K1, (P1, K1) across.

Rows 15-27: Work in Seed Stitch across to marker **(see Seed Stitch, page 77)**, work in Stockinette Stitch across to next marker **(see Stockinette Stitch, page 77)**, work in Seed Stitch across.

Row 28: Work in Seed Stitch across to marker, K 11, place marker, K1, (P1, K1) across to last 20 sts, place marker, knit across to next marker, work in Seed Stitch across.

Rows 29-53: (Work in Seed Stitch across to next marker, work in Stockinette Stitch across to next marker) twice, work in Seed Stitch across.

Row 54: Work in Seed Stitch across to marker, knit across to next marker, K1, (P1, K1) 8 times, place marker, K 87, place marker, work in Seed Stitch across to next marker, knit across to next marker, work in Seed Stitch across.

Rows 55-67: (Work in Seed Stitch across to next marker, work in Stockinette Stitch across to next marker) 3 times, work in Seed Stitch across.

Row 68: Work in Seed Stitch across to marker, knit across to next marker, work in Seed Stitch across to next marker, K 11, place marker, K1, (P1, K1) across to within 11 sts of next marker, place marker, knit across to next marker, work in Seed Stitch across to next marker, knit across to next marker, work in Seed Stitch across.

Rows 69-93: (Work in Seed Stitch across to next marker, work in Stockinette Stitch across to next marker) 4 times, work in Seed Stitch across.

Row 94: (Work in Seed Stitch across to next marker, knit across to next marker) twice, K1, (P1, K1) 8 times, place marker, K 31, place marker, (work in Seed Stitch across to next marker, knit across to next marker) twice, work in Seed Stitch across.

Rows 95-107: (Work in Seed Stitch across to next marker, work in Stockinette Stitch across to next marker) 5 times, work in Seed Stitch across.

Row 108: Work in Seed Stitch across to marker, (knit across to next marker, work in Seed Stitch across to next marker) twice, K 11, place marker, K1, (P1, K1) 4 times, place marker, knit across to next marker, (work in Seed Stitch across to next marker, knit across to next marker) twice, work in Seed Stitch across.

Rows 109-197: (Work in Seed Stitch across to next marker, work in Stockinette Stitch across to next marker) 6 times, work in Seed Stitch across.

Row 198: Work in Seed Stitch across to marker, (knit across to next marker, work in Seed Stitch across to next marker) twice, K 31 removing next 2 markers, (work in Seed Stitch across to next marker, knit across to next marker) twice, work in Seed Stitch across.

Rows 199-211: Repeat Rows 95-107.

Continued on page 74

SIMPLY RIDGES

Your little darling is sure to have pleasant dreams under this easy-to-make throw.
Shown here in a netural shade, it would make an attractive wrap in any color.

Finished Size: 35" x 45"

MATERIALS
Worsted Weight Yarn:
20 ounces, (570 grams, 1,305 yards)
29" Circular knitting needle, size 11 (8.00 mm)
or size needed for gauge
Markers

GAUGE: Rows 1-22 = 5" x 5" x 6³/₄"
corner triangle
In pattern, 14 sts and 20 rows = 4"

Afghan is made by forming lower corner triangle first.

AFGHAN
Cast on one st.

Row 1: Increase *(see Increases, page 77)*: 2 sts.

Row 2: Increase, K1: 3 sts.

Rows 3-6: Increase, knit across: 7 sts.

Rows 7-159: K3, YO *(Fig. 4a, page 77)*, knit across: 160 sts.

Place a marker on right edge as decrease edge and on left edge as increase edge *(see Markers, page 76)*.

Row 160: K2, K2 tog *(Fig. 5, page 78)*, YO, K2 tog, knit across: 159 sts.

Row 161: K3, YO, knit across: 160 sts.

Repeat Rows 160 and 161 until increase edge measures approximately 45", ending by working Row 161: 160 sts.

Decrease Row: K2, K2 tog, YO, K2 tog, knit across: 159 sts.

Repeat Decrease Row until 7 sts remain on needle

Next 5 Rows: K2 tog, knit across: 2 sts.

Last Row: K2 tog: one st.

Finish off.

Design by John Feddersen, Jr.

With rows of kitty cats to provide your little sweetie with constant companionship, this delightful afghan will become an everyday favorite.

Finished Size: 37¹/₂" x 40"

MATERIALS

Worsted Weight Yarn:
    White - 12 ounces, (340 grams, 825 yards)
    Yellow - 5 ounces, (140 grams, 345 yards)
    Green - 10 yards
24" Circular knitting needle, size 10 (6.00 mm)
    or size needed for gauge
Cable needle
Yarn needle

GAUGE: In Stockinette Stitch,
        16 sts and 22 rows = 4"

STITCH GUIDE

ADDING NEW STITCHES
Insert right needle into st as if to **knit**, YO and pull up a loop **(Fig. A)**, slip loop just worked back onto left needle **(Fig. B)**. Repeat for required number of stitches.

Fig. A   **Fig. B**

 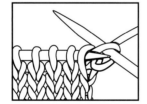

CABLE 4 BACK *(abbreviated C4B)*
(uses 4 sts)
Slip next 2 sts onto cable needle and hold in **back** of work, K2 from left needle, K2 from cable needle.

CABLE 4 FRONT *(abbreviated C4F)*
(uses 4 sts)
Slip next 2 sts onto cable needle and hold in **front** of work, K2 from left needle, K2 from cable needle.

AFGHAN

With White, cast on 150 sts.

Row 1 (Right side)**:** (K1, P1) across.

Row 2: (P1, K1) across.

Rows 3-12: Repeat Rows 1 and 2, 5 times.

Row 13: (K1, P1) 5 times, knit across to last 9 sts, P1, (K1, P1) across.

Row 14: (P1, K1) 5 times, purl across to last 9 sts, K1, (P1, K1) across.

Rows 15-28: Repeat Rows 13 and 14, 7 times.

Row 29: With Yellow, knit across.

Row 30: (P1, K1) across.

Row 31: (K1, P1) across.

Row 32-36: Repeat Rows 30 and 31 twice, then repeat Row 30 once **more**.

Row 37: With White, knit across.

Row 38: (P1, K1) 5 times, purl across to last 9 sts, K1, (P1, K1) across.

Row 39: (K1, P1) 5 times, knit across to last 9 sts, P1, (K1, P1) across.

Rows 40-42: Repeat Rows 38 and 39 once, then repeat Row 38 once **more**.

Rows 43-50: Repeat Rows 29-36.

Row 51 (First Kitten Panel)**:** With White, knit across.

Row 52: P1, (K1, P1) 4 times, knit across to last 10 sts, (P1, K1) across.

Row 53: K1, (P1, K1) 4 times, purl across to last 10 sts, (K1, P1) across.

Row 54: P1, (K1, P1) 4 times, knit across to last 10 sts, (P1, K1) across.

When instructed to slip a stitch, always slip as if to **purl** with yarn held **loosely** in **front**.

Row 55: K1, (P1, K1) 4 times, ★ P6, K2, (slip 1, K2) twice; repeat from ★ across to last 15 sts, P5, (K1, P1) across.

Continued on page 75.

SOOTHING RIPPLES

This soothing ripple afghan will offer safe passage as Baby sets sail for Dreamland. You'll admire its snuggly appeal almost as much as your li'l sailor does.

Finished Size: 35" x 40"

MATERIALS
Worsted Weight Yarn:
  White - 8 ounces, (230 grams, 520 yards)
  Blue - 8 ounces, (230 grams, 520 yards)
  Green - 8 ounces, (230 grams, 520 yards)
29" Circular knitting needle, size 11 (8.00 mm)
  or size needed for gauge
Crochet hook for fringe

GAUGE: In Stockinette Stitch,
    14 sts and 18 rows = 4"

AFGHAN
With White, cast on 139 sts.

Row 1 (Right side)**:** K2, ★ K2 tog *(Fig. 5, page 78)*, K5, YO *(Fig. 4a, page 77)*, K1, YO, K5, **[**slip 1, K1, PSSO *(Fig. 10, page 78)***]**; repeat from ★ across to last 2 sts, K2.

Row 2: K2, purl across to last 2 sts, K2.

Row 3: K2, ★ K2 tog, K5, YO, K1, YO, K5, slip 1, K1, PSSO; repeat from ★ across to last 2 sts, K2.

Row 4: K2, purl across to last 2 sts, K2.

Rows 5-10: Repeat Rows 3 and 4, 3 times.

Row 11: With Blue, K2, ★ K2 tog, K5, YO, K1, YO, K5, slip 1, K1, PSSO; repeat from ★ across to last 2 sts, K2.

Row 12: K2, purl across to last 2 sts, K2.

Rows 13-20: Repeat Rows 11 and 12, 4 times.

Row 21: With Green, K2, ★ K2 tog, K5, YO, K1, YO, K5, slip 1, K1, PSSO; repeat from ★ across to last 2 sts, K2.

Row 22: K2, purl across to last 2 sts, K2.

Rows 23-30: Repeat Rows 21 and 22, 4 times.

Row 31: With White, K2, ★ K2 tog, K5, YO, K1, YO, K5, slip 1, K1, PSSO; repeat from ★ across to last 2 sts, K2.

Row 32: K2, purl across to last 2 sts, K2.

Rows 33-40: Repeat Rows 31 and 32, 4 times.

Rows 41-160: Repeat Rows 11-40, 4 times.

Bind off all sts in **knit**.

Holding eight 16" lengths of White yarn together, add fringe to each point and between points across short edges of Afghan through Step 1 *(see Fringe, page 80)*.

Design by John Feddersen, Jr.

A FROSTY FRIEND

Chase away winter's chill with this frosty friend. His warm personality will keep your baby nice and toasty while the North wind blows.

Finished Size: 30" x 43"

MATERIALS

Worsted Weight Yarn:
    White - 6 ounces, (170 grams, 395 yards)
    Pink - 5 ounces, (140 grams, 330 yards)
    Blue - 1/2 ounce, (15 grams, 35 yards)
    Black - 1/2 ounce, (15 grams, 35 yards)
29" Circular knitting needle, size 10 (6.00 mm)
    or size needed for gauge

GAUGE: In Stockinette Stitch,
        16 sts and 22 rows = 4"

Row gauge is important in this design.

AFGHAN

With White, cast on 120 sts.

Rows 1-13: Knit across.

Row 14 (Right side)**:** K8 (Border), drop White; with Pink *(Fig. 15, page 79)*, knit across to last 8 sts, drop Pink; with second White, knit across (Border).

Row 15: K8, drop White; with Pink, purl across to last 8 sts, drop Pink; with second White, knit across.

Rows 16-33: Repeat Rows 14 and 15, 9 times.

Row 34: K8, drop White; with Pink, K 46, drop Pink; with White, K 21, drop White; with Pink, K 37, drop Pink; with White, knit across.

Rows 35-208: Following Charts, pages 70 and 71, continue to work in Stockinette Stitch *(see Stockinette Stitch, page 76)*, working first and last 8 sts in Garter Stitch *(see Garter Stitch, page 77)*.

Row 209: K8, drop White; with Pink, purl across to last 8 sts, drop Pink; with White, knit across.

Row 210: K8, drop White; with Pink, knit across to last 8 sts, drop Pink; with White, knit across.

Rows 211-229: Repeat Rows 209 and 210, 9 times; then repeat Row 209 once **more**.

Rows 230-242: With White, knit across.

Bind off all sts in **knit**.

Design by Lorraine White.

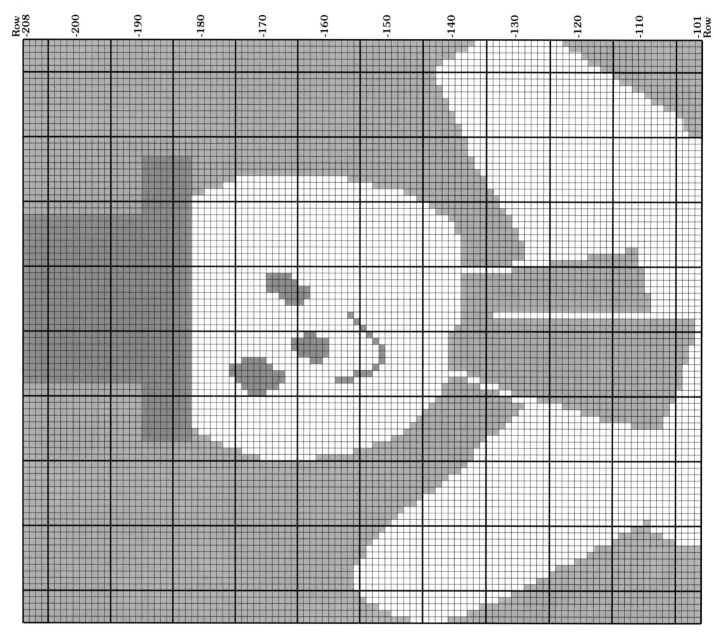

Row -208   -200   -190   -180   -170   -160   -150   -140   -130   -120   -110   -101 Row

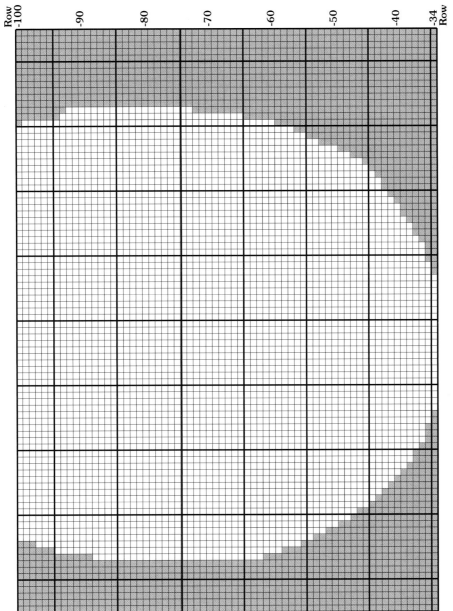

On **right** side rows, work Charts from **right** to **left**;
on **wrong** side rows, work from **left** to **right**.

PRECIOUS IN PINK

continued from page 4.

Row 48: K 15, (SSK, YO) 3 times, K1 tbl, YO, (K2 tog, YO) twice, slip 1, K2 tog, PSSO, YO, (SSK, YO) twice, K1 tbl, (YO, K2 tog) 3 times, ★ K 10, (SSK, YO) 3 times, K1 tbl, YO, (K2 tog, YO) twice, slip 1, K2 tog, PSSO, YO, (SSK, YO) twice, K1 tbl, (YO, K2 tog) 3 times; repeat from ★ 2 times **more**, K 15.

Row 50: K 16, increase, (YO, SSK) twice, K3 tog *(Fig. 7, page 78)*, with left needle bring second st on right needle over first st and off the needle, YO, K2 tog, YO, increase, K1, increase, (YO, SSK) twice, K3 tog, with left needle bring second st on right needle over first st and off the needle, YO, K2 tog, YO, increase, ★ K 12, increase, (YO, SSK) twice, K3 tog, with left needle bring second st on right needle over first st and off the needle, YO, K2 tog, YO, increase, K1, increase, (YO, SSK) twice, K3 tog, with left needle bring second st on right needle over first st and off the needle, YO, K2 tog, YO, increase; repeat from ★ 2 times **more**, K 16.

Row 52: K 18, increase, YO, SSK, K3 tog, with left needle bring second st on right needle over first st and off the needle, YO, increase, K5, increase, YO, SSK, K3 tog, with left needle bring second st on right needle over first st and off the needle, YO, increase, ★ K 16, increase, YO, SSK, K3 tog, with left needle bring second st on right needle over first st and off the needle, YO, increase, K5, increase, YO, SSK, K3 tog, with left needle bring second st on right needle over first st and off the needle, YO, increase; repeat from ★ 2 times **more**, K 18.

Row 54: K 20, ★ WYB slip 3 sts as if to **purl**, WYF slip same 3 sts back onto left needle, WYB knit same 3 sts, K9, WYB slip 3 sts as if to **purl**, WYF slip same 3 sts back onto left needle, WYB knit same 3 sts, K 20; repeat from ★ across.

Row 55: K5, purl across to last 5 sts, K5.

Row 56: Knit across.

Rows 57-65: Repeat Rows 55 and 56, 4 times; then repeat Row 55 once **more**.

Rows 66-284: Repeat Rows 22-65, 4 times; then repeat Rows 22-64 once **more**.

Row 285: K5, P 10, ★ P2 tog *(Fig. 8, page 78)*, P 12; repeat from ★ across to last 5 sts, K5: 150 sts.

Rows 286-294: Knit across.

Bind off all sts in **knit**.

Design by Brooke Shellflower.

WINTRY WARMER

continued from page 48.

Row 22: K1, (P1, K1) twice, P2, slip 1, K2, PSSO, P2, ★ K1, K2 tog, YO, K4, YO, SSK, K1, P2, slip 1, K2, PSSO, P2; repeat from ★ across to last 5 sts, K1, (P1, K1) twice: 128 sts.

Row 23: (K1, P1) twice, K3, P2, ★ K2, P 10, K2, P2; repeat from ★ across to last 7 sts, K3, (P1, K1) twice.

Row 24: K1, (P1, K1) twice, P2, K1, YO, K1, P2, ★ K2 tog, YO, K1, K2 tog, YO twice, SSK, K1, YO, SSK, P2, K1, YO, K1, P2; repeat from ★ across to last 5 sts, K1, (P1, K1) twice: 136 sts.

Row 25: (K1, P1) twice, K3, P3, ★ K2, P4, K1, P5, K2, P3; repeat from ★ across to last 7 sts, K3, (P1, K1) twice.

Row 26: K1, (P1, K1) twice, P2, slip 1, K2, PSSO, P2, ★ K2, YO, SSK, K2, K2 tog, YO, K2, P2, slip 1, K2, PSSO, P2; repeat from ★ across to last 5 sts, K1, (P1, K1) twice: 128 sts.

Row 27: (K1, P1) twice, K3, P2, ★ K2, P 10, K2, P2; repeat from ★ across to last 7 sts, K3, (P1, K1) twice.

Row 28: K1, (P1, K1) twice, P2, K1, YO, K1, P2, ★ K3, YO, SSK, K2 tog, YO, K3, P2, K1, YO, K1, P2; repeat from ★ across to last 5 sts, K1, (P1, K1) twice: 136 sts.

Row 29: (K1, P1) twice, K3, P3, ★ K2, P 10, K2, P3; repeat from ★ across to last 7 sts, K3, (P1, K1) twice.

Repeat Rows 10-29 for pattern until Afghan measures approximately 41" from cast on edge, ending by working Row 21.

Next Row (Decrease row)**:** (K1, P1) twice, K2 tog, (P1, K1) across: 135 sts.

Last 6 Rows: K1, (P1, K1) across.

Bind off all sts in pattern.

Design by Rachel J. Terrill.

CLASSIC RIPPLES

continued from page 54.

TRIM

With **right** side facing, using crochet hook, and working across long edge of Afghan Body, join White with sc in end of first row; sc in next row and in each row across working over the White carried along the edge; finish off.

Repeat across second edge.

Design by Meredith Montross.

FOR A BONNY BABE

continued from page 58.

Row 17 (Increase row)**:** K1, (P1, K1) 7 times, increase *(see Increases, page 77)*, ★ [K1, (P1, K1) 4 times, increase] twice, K1, (P1, K1) 11 times, increase; repeat from ★ once **more**, [K1, (P1, K1) 4 times, increase] twice, K1, (P1, K1) across: 148 sts.

Row 18 (Right side)**:** K1, (P1, K1) 5 times, place marker *(see Markers, page 76)*, K1, P2, K4, P2, K1, P4, K4, P4, K1, P2, K4, P2, K1, place marker, ★ K1, (P1, K1) 7 times, place marker, K1, P2, K4, P2, K1, P4, K4, P4, K1, P2, K4, P2, K1, place marker; repeat from ★ once **more**, K1, (P1, K1) across.

Row 19: K1, (P1, K1) 5 times, P1, K2, P4, K2, P1, K4, P4, K4, P1, K2, P4, K2, P1, ★ K1, (P1, K1) 7 times, P1, K2, P4, K2, P1, K4, P4, K4, P1, K2, P4, K2, P1; repeat from ★ once **more**, K1, (P1, K1) across.

Row 20: K1 (P1, K1) 5 times, work Row 1 of Small Cable, work Row 1 of Cabled Diamond, work Row 1 of Small Cable, ★ K1, (P1, K1) 7 times, work Row 1 of Small Cable, work Row 1 of Cabled Diamond, work Row 1 of Small Cable; repeat from ★ once **more**, K1, (P1, K1) across.

Row 21: K1, (P1, K1) 5 times, work Row 2 of Small Cable, work Row 2 of Cabled Diamond, work Row 2 of Small Cable, ★ K1, (P1, K1) 7 times, work Row 2 of Small Cable, work Row 2 of Cabled Diamond, work Row 2 of Small Cable; repeat from ★ once **more**, K1, (P1, K1) across.

Row 22: K1, (P1, K1) 5 times, work next row of Small Cable, work next row of Cabled Diamond, work same row of Small Cable, ★ K1, (P1, K1) 7 times, work same row of Small Cable, work same row of Cabled Diamond, work same row of Small Cable; repeat from ★ once **more**, K1, (P1, K1) across.

Repeat Row 22 for pattern until Afghan measures approximately 30" from cast on edge, ending by working Row 10 of Cabled Diamond.

Next Row (Decrease row)**:** K1, (P1, K1) 7 times, P2 tog *(Fig. 8, page 78)*, [K1, (P1, K1) 4 times, P2 tog] twice, ★ K1, (P1, K1) 11 times, P2 tog, [K1, (P1, K1) 4 times, P2 tog] twice; repeat from ★ once **more**, K1, (P1, K1) across: 139 sts.

Last 16 Rows: K1, (P1, K1) across.

Bind off all sts in pattern.

Design by Marion Graham.

PRETTY POSIES

continued from page 60.

Row 212: (Work in Seed Stitch across to next marker, knit across to next marker) twice, work 65 sts in Seed Stitch removing next 2 markers, knit across to next marker, work in Seed Stitch across to next marker, knit across to next marker, work in Seed Stitch across.

Rows 213-237: (Work in Seed Stitch across to next marker, work in Stockinette Stitch across to next marker) 4 times, work in Seed Stitch across.

Row 238: Work in Seed Stitch across to marker, knit across to next marker, work in Seed Stitch across to next marker, K 87 removing next 2 markers, work in Seed Stitch across to next marker, knit across to next marker, work in Seed Stitch across.

Rows 239-251: (Work in Seed Stitch across to next marker, work in Stockinette Stitch across to next marker) 3 times, work in Seed Stitch across.

Row 252: Work in Seed Stitch across to marker, knit across to next marker, work in Seed Stitch across to last 20 sts removing next 2 markers, knit across to next marker, work in Seed Stitch across.

Rows 253-277: (Work in Seed Stitch across to next marker, work in Stockinette Stitch across to next marker) twice, work in Seed Stitch across.

Row 278: Work in Seed Stitch across to marker, knit across to last 9 sts removing next 2 markers, work in Seed Stitch across.

Rows 279-291: Work in Seed Stitch across to marker, work in Stockinette Stitch across to next marker, work in Seed Stitch across.

Row 292: Work in Seed Stitch across, removing remaining 2 markers.

Rows 293-304: K1, (P1, K1) across.

Bind off all sts in pattern.

FINISHING

Using photo, page 61, and Chart as a guide for placement, add 12-petal Lazy Daisy Stitch flowers in colors indicated to **right** side of Afghan **(Fig. 19, page 80)**. Using Green, add four 1-petal Lazy Daisy Stitch leaves to each flower. Using Yellow, add 3 French Knots to center of each flower **(Fig. 18, page 80)**.

Design by Marion Graham.

CHART

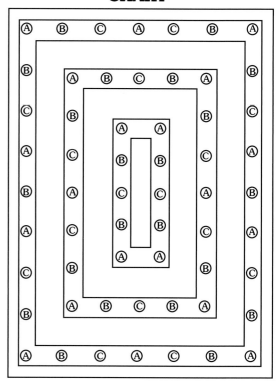

KEY

A = Pink   B = Blue   C = Lavender

"PURR-FECT" CONTENTMENT

continued from page 64.

Row 56: P1, (K1, P1) 4 times, (K6, P8) across to last 15 sts, K5, (P1, K1) across.

Row 57: K1, (P1, K1) 4 times, P6, K2, (slip 1, K2) twice, ★ P6, K2, slip 1, K1, add 10 sts onto left needle (keeping tail to front of work) *(Figs. A & B, page 64)*, do **not** turn; bind off 10 sts (counting each st as you bind off), slip 1, K2, P6, K2, (slip 1, K2) twice; repeat from ★ 3 times **more**, P5, (K1, P1) across.

Row 58: P1, (K1, P1) 4 times, (K6, P8) across to last 15 sts, K5, (P1, K1) across.

Rows 59-66: Repeat Rows 55 and 56, 4 times.

Row 67: K1, (P1, K1) 4 times, ★ P6, work C4B, work C4F; repeat from ★ across to last 15 sts, P5, (K1, P1) across.

Row 68: P1, (K1, P1) 4 times, (K6, P8) across to last 15 sts, K5, (P1, K1) across.

Row 69: K1, (P1, K1) 4 times, (P6, K8) across to last 15 sts, P5, (K1, P1) across.

Rows 70-72: Repeat Rows 68 and 69 once, then repeat Row 68 once **more**.

Row 73: K1, (P1, K1) 4 times, P5, ★ work C4B, K2, work C4F, P4; repeat from ★ across to last 10 sts, (K1, P1) across.

Row 74: P1, (K1, P1) 4 times, (K6, P1) across to last 15 sts, K5, (P1, K1) across.

Row 75: K1, (P1, K1) 4 times, purl across to last 10 sts, (K1, P1) across.

Row 76: P1, (K1, P1) 4 times, knit across to last 10 sts, (P1, K1) across.

Rows 77 and 78: Repeat Rows 75 and 76.

Rows 79-100: Repeat Rows 29-50.

Row 101: With White, knit across.

Row 102: (P1, K1) 5 times, purl across to last 9 sts, K1, (P1, K1) across.

Rows 103-132: Repeat Rows 13 and 14, 15 times.

Rows 133-154: Repeat Rows 29-50.

Row 155 (Second Kitten Panel)**:** With White, knit across.

Row 156: P1, (K1, P1) 4 times, knit across to last 10 sts, (P1, K1) across.

Row 157: K1, (P1, K1) 4 times, purl across to last 10 sts, (K1, P1) across.

Row 158: P1, (K1, P1) 4 times, (K6, P1) across to last 15 sts, K5, (P1, K1) across.

Row 159: K1, (P1, K1) 4 times, P5, ★ work C4F, K2, work C4B, P4; repeat from ★ across to last 10 sts, (K1, P1) across.

Row 160: P1, (K1, P1) 4 times, (K6, P8) across to last 15 sts, K5, (P1, K1) across.

Row 161: K1, (P1, K1) 4 times, (P6, K8) across to last 15 sts, P5, (K1, P1) across.

Rows 162-164: Repeat Rows 160 and 161 once, then repeat Row 160 once **more**.

Row 165: K1, (P1, K1) 4 times, ★ P6, work C4F, work C4B; repeat from ★ across to last 15 sts, P5, (K1, P1) across.

Row 166: P1, (K1, P1) 4 times, (K6, P8) across to last 15 sts, K5, (P1, K1) across.

Row 167: K1, (P1, K1) 4 times, ★ P6, K2, (slip 1, K2) twice; repeat from ★ across to last 15 sts, P5, (K1, P1) across.

Rows 168-174: Repeat Rows 166 and 167, 3 times; then repeat Row 166 once **more**.

Row 175: K1, (P1, K1) 4 times, P6, K2, (slip 1, K2) twice, ★ P6, K2, slip 1, K1, add 10 sts onto left needle (keeping tail to front of work), do **not** turn; bind off 10 sts, (counting each st as you bind off), slip 1, K2, P6, K2, (slip 1, K2) twice; repeat from ★ 3 times **more**, P5, (K1, P1) across.

Rows 176 and 177: Repeat Rows 166 and 167.

Rows 178-182: Repeat Rows 156 and 157 twice, then repeat Row 156 once **more**.

Rows 183-206: Repeat Rows 79-102.

Rows 207-222: Repeat Rows 13 and 14, 8 times.

Rows 223-234: Repeat Rows 1-12.

Bind off all sts in pattern.

FINISHING
With Green and using photo, page 65, as a guide for placement, add features and neckties.

Design by Barbara Boulton.

GENERAL INSTRUCTIONS

ABBREVIATIONS

C2B	Cable 2 Back
C2F	Cable 2 Front
C4B	Cable 4 Back
C4F	Cable 4 Front
K	knit
mm	millimeters
P	purl
PSSO	pass slipped stitch over
P2SSO	pass 2 slipped stitches over
RT	Right Twist
SSK	slip, slip, knit
sc	single crochet(s)
st(s)	stitch(es)
T2B	Twist 2 Back
T2F	Twist 2 Front
tbl	through back loop(s)
tog	together
WYB	with yarn in back
WYF	with yarn in front
YO	yarn over

★ — work instructions following ★ as many **more** times as indicated in addition to the first time.

† to † — work all instructions from first † to second † **as many** times as specified.

( ) or [ ] — work enclosed instructions **as many** times as specified by the number immediately following **or** work all enclosed instructions in the stitch or space indicated **or** contains explanatory remarks.

colon (:) — the number(s) given after a colon at the end of a row denote(s) the number of stitches you should have on that row.

GAUGE

Exact gauge is **essential** for proper size. Before beginning your Afghan, make a sample swatch in the yarn and needle specified. After completing the swatch, measure it, counting your stitches and rows carefully. If your swatch is larger or smaller than specified, **make another, changing needle size to get the correct gauge**. Keep trying until you find the size needles that will give you the specified gauge. Once proper gauge is obtained, measure width of Afghan approximately every 3" to be sure gauge remains consistent.

YARN

The Afghans shown can be made with any yarn in the weight specified, as long as the correct gauge can be obtained.

A Fingering Weight Yarn is any yarn that lists gauge on the label as 7 sts = 1" in Stockinette Stitch.

A Sport Weight Yarn is any yarn that lists gauge on the label as 6 sts = 1" in Stockinette Stitch.

A Worsted Weight Yarn is any yarn that lists gauge on the label as 5 sts = 1" in Stockinette Stitch.

It is best to refer to the yardage to determine how many balls or skeins to purchase. Remember, in order for your Afghan to be the correct size, it is not the brand of yarn that matters, but the GAUGE that is important.

MARKERS

As a convenience to you, we have used markers to help distinguish the beginning of a pattern or edge of a row. Place markers as instructed. You may use purchased markers or tie a length of contrasting color yarn around the needle. When you reach a marker on each row, slip it from the left needle to the right needle; remove it when no longer needed.

KNITTING NEEDLES																
U.S.	0	1	2	3	4	5	6	7	8	9	10	10½	11	13	15	17
English/U.K.	13	12	11	10	9	8	7	6	5	4	3	2	1	00	000	---
Metric - mm	2.00	2.25	2.75	3.25	3.50	3.75	4.00	4.50	5.00	5.50	6.00	6.50	8.00	9.00	10.00	12.75

BASIC PATTERN STITCHES
STOCKINETTE STITCH

Knit one row or number of stitches indicated (right side), purl one row or number of stitches indicated. The knit side is smooth and flat (*Fig. 1a*), and the purl side is bumpy (*Fig. 1b*).

Fig. 1a

Fig. 1b

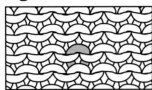

GARTER STITCH

Knit every row. Two rows of knitting make one horizontal ridge in your fabric (*Fig. 2*).

Fig. 2

SEED STITCH

Knit the purl stitches and purl the knit stitches as they face you.

WORKING THROUGH BACK LOOPS

Knit: With yarn in back, insert the right needle into the **back** of the next stitch from **front** to **back** (*Fig. 3a*) and knit it.

Purl: With yarn in front, insert the right needle into the **back** of the next stitch from **back** to **front** (*Fig. 3b*) and purl it.

Fig. 3a

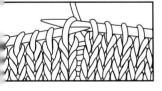

Fig. 3b

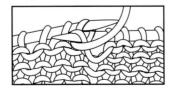

INCREASES

Increases are made by working into the front **and** into the back of the next stitch.

INCREASING EVENLY ACROSS A ROW

Add one to the number of increases required and divide that number into the number of stitches on the needle. Subtract one from the result and the new number is the approximate number of stitches to be worked **between** each increase. Adjust the number as needed.

YARN OVERS

After a knit stitch, before a knit stitch
Bring the yarn forward **between** the needles, then back **over** the top of the right hand needle, so that it is now in position to knit the next stitch (*Fig. 4a*).

Fig. 4a

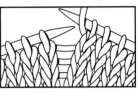

After a purl stitch, before a purl stitch
Take yarn **over** the right hand needle to the back, then forward **under** it, so that it is now in position to purl the next stitch (*Fig. 4b*).

Fig. 4b

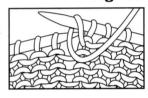

After a knit stitch, before a purl stitch
Bring yarn forward **between** the needles, then back **over** the top of the right hand needle and forward **between** the needles again, so that it is now in position to purl the next stitch (*Fig. 4c*).

Fig. 4c

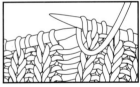

After a purl stitch, before a knit stitch
Take yarn **over** right hand needle to the back, so that it is now in position to knit the next stitch (*Fig. 4d*).

Fig. 4d

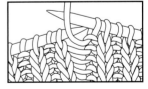

DECREASES

KNIT 2 TOGETHER (abbreviated K2 tog)

Insert the right needle into the **front** of the first two stitches on the left needle as if to **knit** (*Fig. 5*), then knit them together.

Fig. 5

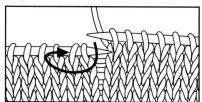

KNIT 2 TOGETHER THROUGH THE BACK LOOP

(abbreviated K2 tog tbl)

Insert the right needle into the **back** of the first two stitches on the left needle from **front** to **back** (*Fig. 6*), then knit them together.

Fig. 6

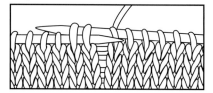

KNIT 3 TOGETHER (abbreviated K3 tog)

Insert the right needle into the **front** of the first three stitches on the left needle as if to **knit** (*Fig. 7*), then knit them together.

Fig. 7

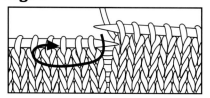

PURL 2 TOGETHER (abbreviated P2 tog)

Insert the right needle into the **front** of the first two stitches on the left needle as if to **purl** (*Fig. 8*), then purl them together.

Fig. 8

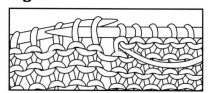

PURL 2 TOGETHER THROUGH THE BACK LOOP

(abbreviated P2 tog tbl)

Insert the right needle into the **back** of both stitches from **back** to **front** (*Fig. 9*), then purl them together.

Fig. 9

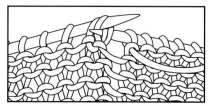

SLIP 1, KNIT 1, PASS SLIPPED STITCH OVER

(abbreviated slip 1, K1, PSSO)

Slip one stitch as if to **knit**. Knit the next stitch. With the left needle, bring the slipped stitch over the knit stitch (*Fig. 10*) and off the needle.

Fig. 10

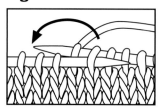

SLIP 1, KNIT 2, PASS SLIPPED STITCH OVER

(abbreviated slip 1, K2, PSSO)

Slip one stitch as if to **knit**. Knit the next two stitches. With the left needle, bring the slipped stitch over the two knit stitches (*Fig. 11*) and off the needle.

Fig. 11

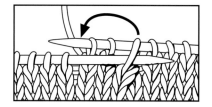

SLIP 1, KNIT 2 TOGETHER, PASS SLIPPED STITCH OVER
(abbreviated slip 1, K2 tog, PSSO)
Slip one stitch as if to **knit** *(Fig. 12a)*, then knit the next two stitches together. With the left needle, bring the slipped stitch over the stitch just made *(Fig. 12b)* and off the needle.

Fig. 12a

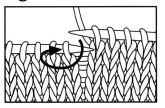

Fig. 12b

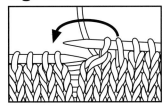

SLIP, SLIP, KNIT *(abbreviated SSK)*
With yarn in back of work, separately slip two stitches as if to **knit** *(Fig. 13a)*. Insert the **left** needle into the **front** of both slipped stitches *(Fig. 13b)* and knit them together *(Fig. 13c)*.

Fig. 13a

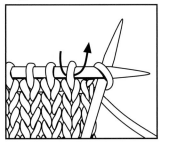

Fig. 13b

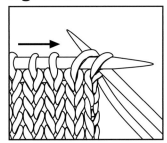

Fig. 13c

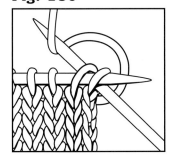

SLIP, SLIP, KNIT 1, PASS 2 SLIPPED STITCHES OVER
(abbreviated slip, slip, K1, P2SSO)
With yarn in back, separately slip two stitches as if to **knit** *(Fig. 14a)*, then knit the next stitch. With the left needle, bring both slipped stitches over the knit stitch *(Fig. 14b)* and off the needle.

Fig. 14a

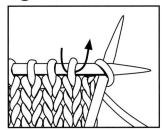

Fig. 14b

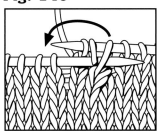

CHANGING COLORS
When changing colors, always pick up the new color yarn from beneath the dropped yarn and keep the color which has just been worked to the left *(Fig. 15)*. This will prevent holes in the finished piece.

Fig. 15

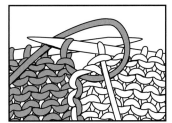

FRINGE

After completing Step(s) specified in individual instructions, lay Afghan flat on a hard surface and trim the ends.

Cut a piece of cardboard 8" wide and half as long as specified in individual instructions for strands. Wind the yarn **loosely** and **evenly** around the cardboard lengthwise until the card is filled, then cut across one end; repeat as needed.

Step 1: Hold together as many strands of yarn as specified for the finished fringe; fold in half. With **wrong** side facing and using a crochet hook, draw the folded end up through a stitch and pull the loose ends through the folded end *(Fig. 16a)*; draw the knot up **tightly** *(Fig. 16b)*. Repeat spacing as desired.

Step 2: Divide each group in half and knot together with half of next group *(Fig. 16c)*.

Step 3: Separate each group in same manner and knot again *(Fig. 16d)*.

Fig. 16a

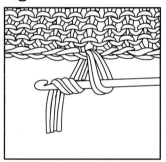

Fig. 16b

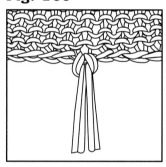

Fig. 16c

Fig. 16d

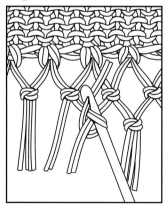

EMBROIDERY
BULLION KNOT

Bring needle up at 1. Wrap yarn around the needle number of times indicated and insert needle at 2, holding end of yarn with non-stitching fingers *(Fig. 17)*. Tighten knot; then pull needle through, holding yarn until it must be released.

Fig. 17

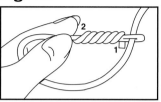

FRENCH KNOT

Bring needle up at 1. Wrap yarn desired number of times around needle and insert needle at 2, holding end of yarn with non-stitching fingers *(Fig. 18)*. Tighten knot; then pull needle through, holding yarn until it must be released.

Fig. 18

LAZY DAISY STITCH

Make all loops equal in length. Come up at 1 and make a counterclockwise loop with the yarn. Go down at 1 and come up at 2, keeping the yarn below the point of the needle *(Fig. 19)*. Secure loop by bringing thread over loop and down at 3. Repeat for the desired number of petals or leaves.

Fig. 19

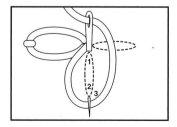

Afghans made and instructions tested by Anitta Armstrong, Beverly Burkhalter, Mike Cates, June Clevenger, Lee Ellis, Raymelle Greening, Kathleen Hardy, Kay Meadors, Peggy Pierpaoli, Dale Potter, Donna Soellner, Margaret Taverner, and Carol Thompson.